Liturgies for Christian Unity

Liturgies for Christian Unity

The First Hundred Years

edited by the Faith and Witness Commission
of the Canadian Council of Churches

Foreword by the Most Rev. Michael G. Peers

© 2008 Novalis, Saint Paul University, Ottawa, Canada

Cover design and layout: Dominique Pelland
Cover image: © Gene Plaisted
Inside images: © Jupiter Images, p. 36, 72, 92; © Jean-Paul Picard, p. 52; © W. P. Wittman, p. 106; © Sam, p. 128; © Cléo, p. 150.

Business Offices:

Novalis Publishing Inc.
10 Lower Spadina Avenue, Suite 400
Toronto, Ontario, Canada
M5V 2Z2

Novalis Publishing Inc.
4475 Frontenac Street
Montréal, Québec, Canada
H2H 2S2

Phone: 1-800-387-7164
Fax: 1-800-204-4140
E-mail: books@novalis.ca
www.novalis.ca

Library and Archives Canada Cataloguing in Publication

Liturgies for Christian unity : the first hundred years, 1908-2008 / edited by the Faith and Witness Commission of the Canadian Council of Churches.

Includes bibliographical references.

ISBN 978-2-89507-958-3

1. Week of Prayer for Christian Unity. 2. Liturgies. 3. Ecumenical movement–Prayers and devotions. I. Canadian Council of Churches. Commission on Faith and Witness.

BV186.7.F35 2008   280'.042   C2007-907563-0

Printed in Canada.

Texts from the World Council of Churches, Graymoor, and Centre Unité Chrétienne are reprinted by permission.

All rights reserved. No part of this publication may be reproduced, stored in a retrieval system, or transmitted in any form, or by any means, electronic, mechanical, photocopying, recording, or otherwise, without the written permission of the publisher.

We acknowledge the financial support of the Government of Canada through the Book Publishing Industry Development Program (BPIDP) for our publishing activities.

5   4   3   2   1   12   11   10   09   08

Contents

Letter from the Graymoor Friars 7

Letter from the Canadian Council of Churches 8

Foreword by the Most Rev. Michael G. Peers 9

Introduction 11

Into Christ's Own Prayer: The Early Development of the Week of Prayer
      for Christian Unity 13

The First Four Decades 37

The 1950s 53

The 1960s 73

The 1970s 93

The 1980s 107

The 1990s 129

2000 and onwards 151

Epilogue 171

Acknowledgments 173

Hymns to Celebrate 100 Years of the Week of Prayer for Christian Unity 176

Subject Index 183

Scripture Index 193

Catholic Pastoral Centre
1155 Yonge Street
Toronto, Ontario
M4T 1W2

Dear Friends in Christ,

One hundred years within a span of more than two thousand years can sometimes go unnoticed. A century of Prayer for Christian Unity, however, cannot occur without remembrance, acknowledgment and celebration.

The materials gathered here leave the fingerprints of many who have given of their time, talent, substance and opportunity to be a beacon of hope in pursuit of the fulfillment of the prayer of Jesus to the Father "that all may be one … so that the world may believe" (Jn. 17:21).

Among those fingerprints we find ecumenical pioneers such as Rev. Paul Wattson of Graymoor and Abbé Paul Couturier in France, both of whom gave vision and direction to the work of church unity in times when it was much less popular to do so. From the earliest days of their ministry, both recognized the central ingredient of Christian prayer as the handmaid in all efforts put forth for church unity. To this day we draw from their legacy. The formation of the World, National and Canadian Councils of Churches, the occurrence of the Second Vatican Council, the manner and means by which Christians now respect and partner with one another, and a host of other landmark achievements are the fruits of prayer and the determined efforts of all who feel the pain of those obstacles that continue to divide Christendom.

Prayer has served to awaken within the Christian world a consciousness that division within itself is both a contradiction and a scandal that weakens the preaching of the gospel. Beginning the second hundred years of prayer for Christian unity, we do so with the same hope and assurance Jesus had when he prayed to his Father. As disciples on the way, there is no turning back.

Rev. Damian MacPherson, SA
Franciscan Friar of the Atonement
Director for Ecumenical and Interfaith Affairs
Archdiocese of Toronto

The Canadian Council of Churches

Le Conseil canadien des Églises

founded in 1944 — fondé en 1944

Dear Sisters and Brothers in Christ,

The words "Let us pray" have resonated long and deep within our tradition. They have called us into community; they have called us both into and out of ourselves; and they have called to us, as people of the Christ who modelled prayer for us, in intimate relationship with our Holy God.

As Christians, we pray. As Christians who believe in the truth of 1 Corinthians 12:12 – "For just as the body is one and has many members, and all the members of the body, though many, are one body, so it is with Christ" – we also resonate with the truth that we are called to pray not only for each other but, according to our traditions, *with* each other. And for 100 years, Christians have been doing just that.

This anthology of the 100 years of materials leading to the Week of Prayer for Christian Unity as we know it today is not only a remarkable achievement, it is a beacon of Christ's light to take us forward into the next 100 years of Christian witness and beyond. Since the 1960s, the Canadian Council of Churches has been putting together the Canadian Week of Prayer for Christian Unity materials. This expression of witness to Christ has always been ecumenical in the make-up of the committee; it has been a deep, challenging and rich experience for all the members of that committee. The commitment to praying together, recognizing all the joys and challenges of such a commitment, has transformed the people and the Christian denominations involved. We have learned, both theologically and in concrete expressions of theology, what unites us and what still causes us to be separate from one another. We have been enabled – as a Council of 21 denominations of the Anglican, Roman Catholic, Protestant, Evangelical and Eastern and Oriental Orthodox traditions, representing approximately 85 percent of the Christians in Canada – to hold a number of public prayer services involving numerous denominations, including both their clergy and laity. We have prayed together publicly, with open invitations to the wide world, for Iraq, for Afghanistan and for the future of ecumenism in Canada as a witness to the diversity in unity of God that we model.

So now that you have this anthology in your hands, the question is rather like the one confronting the disciples after the Resurrection of Christ: "Now what?"

Read the materials. Share them with your congregations and colleagues. Plan a particular way to mark the 100th anniversary of the Week of Prayer for Christian Unity, doing such planning ecumenically, of course.

And pray. Pray through the selections, pray with the selections, pray without ceasing and know that in praying the truth you are called to love and serve the Lord. Thanks be to God!

The Rev. Dr. Karen Hamilton
General Secretary
The Canadian Council of Churches

47 Queen's Park Crescent East, Toronto, Ontario, Canada M5S 2C3 • Tel: 416-972-9494 • 1-866-822-7645
Fax: 416-927-0405 • E-mail/Courrier élect.: admin@ccc-cce.ca • http://www.ccc-cce.ca

Foreword

I am delighted to be invited to write an introduction to this celebratory collection of material from a century of prayer for the unity of Christian people and Christian churches; I write from the point of view of a witness both to the prayer of the worldwide Church and particularly to its impact among Canadian Christians. I also write from the conviction, learned through many experiences, some painful, that unless Christian endeavour takes root locally, its capacity to effect significant change in persons and institutions is weakened.

It was 50 years ago that I, as a theological student, became personally aware of the isolation of Christians from one another. For example, one day another student and I were in the chapel of our college on the campus of the University of Toronto. Two young men in black suits somewhat hesitatingly entered the chapel, and we greeted them. They were Roman Catholic seminarians; it had been suggested to them that they might look at (*not* worship in!) other church buildings, something neither had ever done. When we explained our daily pattern of worship – Eucharist, Morning and Evening Prayer, Compline – they were astonished. They had thought that Protestant worship was just a long sermon and some hymns!

I also became aware from my own experience, and that of several classmates, that there were congregations of Eastern Orthodox immigrants looking to our church for "houseroom." One of our responses was to found a Canadian branch of the Fellowship of St Alban and St Sergius, a body that prays for the unity of Anglican and Orthodox Christians.

From those beginnings of awareness and action, I have been blessed by the opportunity to be involved in ecumenical work in local, regional, national and worldwide arenas. I have prayed and worked for efforts at closer structural links with two major bodies: in the 60s and 70s, the Plan of Union with the United Church of Canada (our efforts were unsuccessful), and in the 80s and 90s, the Waterloo Declaration with the Evangelical Lutheran Church of Canada (a different outcome). For a couple of decades I was a co-presider of meetings of Canadian Roman Catholic and Anglican bishops, and in the first decade of this century I was a member of the Special Commission on the Place of Orthodox Churches in the World Council of Churches.

Canadians have been especially blessed in a number of ways through these years. The distinguished Roman Catholic ecumenist Thomas Ryan, CSP, has observed how often Canadian ecumenical conversation has both arisen from, and also given rise to, deep personal friendship. I am not the only person to have been a beneficiary of that phenomenon.

Canadian churches, as institutions, have adopted for many decades the principle of common social action, especially towards government, wherever that has been possible, and our "coalitions" have been the envy of many other national groupings of Christians.

But a crowning ecumenical experience for me arose as a gift, in a sense, of the late Robert Runcie, Archbishop of Canterbury in the 1980s, during his formal visit to the Canadian church. In his major ecumenical address, in the Montreal Basilica of Notre-Dame, he outlined his perception of our history as Christian communities in Canada. He sketched our movement from the initial stage of "confrontation," then to a time of "coexistence" and now to the point of "cooperation." Finally, he laid before us the challenge, as he saw it, of the inevitable next frontier: "communion." A few weeks after his address, I was invited, as the local Anglican archbishop, to bring official greetings to the 75th anniversary of the Roman Catholic Archdiocese of Regina at a festival Eucharist with 10,000 people in the Agridome. I quoted Dr Runcie's exposition of our common history in Canada and ended with his challenge of moving towards communion. The result was instantaneous – thunderous and sustained applause. I don't know who was more surprised: me or the Roman Catholic bishops.

I have always taken great comfort from that moment; it was a sign that the will towards unity is deeply ingrained where it is most essential – among laypeople.

These classic Canadian ecumenical spheres – personal friendship, social concern, lay conviction – are signs of the "glue" of our relationships, as Desmond Tutu once identified it: "the glue is that we *meet*." The strong affirmation given by the Evangelical Lutheran Church in Canada and the Anglican Church owes much to "meetings" of their constituents from local congregations to national leadership, for prayer, dialogue and meals over more than a decade before intercommunion became a reality.

A hundred years ago, occasions for such profound "meeting" were rare, and prayer may have seemed the only area open. But prayer is not only the best place to begin a journey, it is the ground beneath our feet as we travel and the goal towards which we move – the prayer of Jesus "that all may be one as you, O Father, and I are one."

Most Rev. Michael G. Peers
Primate of the Anglican Church of Canada 1986–2004

Introduction

How the Week of Prayer for Christian Unity Is Celebrated

The Week of Prayer is observed around the world each year, usually between January 18 and 25, the feasts of Saints Peter and Paul. The actual time of celebration may vary; indeed, churches are encouraged to celebrate and pray for Christian unity, and use resource materials, throughout the year. Pentecost is also a popular time in which to highlight the celebration.

This tradition has grown out of a series of movements and gatherings, prompted by the passion and actions of countless individuals who believed and hoped deeply in the unity of Christians. Beginning in 1908, the Octave of Christian Unity was commemorated by the Friars of the Atonement at Graymoor in Garrison, New York. Since 1948, the World Council of Churches has published an annual prayer service for the Week of Prayer for Christian Unity. Since 1968, the Canadian Council of Churches has published its own annual Week of Prayer service.

Kinds of Texts Used in the Week of Prayer

The year's theme, and a focus biblical text, are prepared by an international Joint Committee of the World Council of Churches and the Pontifical Commission for the Promotion of Christian Unity. Each year, a different country hosts the Joint Committee and helps to write the materials; Canada has been the host country on three occasions. National and regional councils of churches work to adapt and add to these resources to their local context. The Canadian resources are produced by an ecumenical committee coordinated by the Commission on Faith and Witness, Canadian Council of Churches.

The collected archives of these liturgical texts, prayers, and reflections – one hundred years' worth – are a treasure chamber. We gathered together as many as we could find, and selected the best gems for this anthology.

In its early years, the Week of Prayer resources focused on the Eight Days themselves: each of the eight days of the "week" or "octave" of the observance included a reflection on a biblical text. The result offered a way to pray and reflect with the Scriptures upon the call to Christian unity.

Over time, prayers, intercessions and an ecumenical worship service based on a particular Scripture quotation were added. By the 1960s, the ecumenical service was the dominant focus, with the Eight Days almost secondary. Later in the twentieth century, other resources were included, such as activities for children and youth, suggested hymns, and artwork. In the twenty-first century, the Eight Days have become more prominent once again.

How to Use This Book

The present selection includes examples of all these types of prayers, liturgies and reflections. It is intended first of all as a pastoral resource to which pastors and liturgical conveners can turn in planning ecumenical services or events. The Subject Index is designed to help in such planning. You may be looking for a particular type of prayer, or working with a specific liturgical or pastoral theme, or with a particular Scripture text; we have tried to be representative in all these aspects.

We have also included prayers and reflections that stand out as particularly beautiful or interesting, or historically relevant. Historical and cultural themes are also included in the index. You may wish simply to leaf through the texts randomly, to pray with them, or to follow their lead in illustrating the movement of prayer and the evolving culture over the past century.

We believe this anthology will also be of great value to the church historian and to the theological student, especially since the ecumenical movement has been such a strong element of both church life and Canadian society over the decades.

We were unable to locate texts for every one of the hundred years. We are also certain there are more texts of Canadian and regional origin than we were able to find. Nevertheless, we have made a solid beginning. If any reader has, or can find, additional texts to help complete these archives, the Canadian Council of Churches would be happy to hear about them.

The editors were moved by the evidence in these texts of a life of prayer that has blown through the ecumenical movement. We noted many times when prayers made in earlier years were later answered, and we can witness to this response. Above all, we hope that this anthology will help renew the call to prayer, and refresh us in the conviction that the Spirit of God is drawing Christians closer together.

Mary Marrocco
Faith and Witness Commission
Canadian Council of Churches

Into Christ's Own Prayer

The Early Development of the
Week of Prayer for Christian Unity

Jennifer Eileen Scully, Anglican Church of Canada

The history of the ecumenical movement, as with all movements, is a complex one. Movements are, by their very nature, organic. They are about the convergence and interplay of a variety of voices. Prayer for Christian unity, and the Week of Prayer in particular, have never been housed in one institution. Rather, they are products of the confluence of several different streams – charismatic individuals, institutional organizers, ecumenical missions and institutions, and the churches themselves.

From the earliest of times, Christians have prayed for the unity of the Church. Liturgies of the Roman, Eastern and Anglican rites and the traditions of the Reformation have all included prayers that Christ's will be done for the unity of the Church. The oneness of Christ's Body, the Church, is a central doctrinal assertion across the traditions. And yet, our understanding of what that "church" is – and where that Body lives – varies. As a result, the scandal of division continues, and Christians have spent centuries praying separately for unity. From time to time movements of prayer have arisen for the healing of these divisions – movements in and by which Christians have been united in the offering of prayer. Differences in the view of what that healing ought to look like have persisted, as have differences of opinion about what "unity" will look like; those differences have at times provoked further scandal. Nevertheless, *because* the stream of Christ's own prayer continues, the prayers of Christians have been drawn together into this stream. Christ's own prayer is that we may be one, even as Christ and God the Father and Creator are one in the Holy Spirit.

Today, the Week of Prayer for Christian Unity tradition invites Christians everywhere to join in the prayer of Christ. We know that the goal of unity is not ours to be accomplished; it is the work of God already offered. We are called to offer ourselves into the prayer of Christ. That Christians of diverse traditions have grown into this awareness is the work of the Holy Spirit, and is due in large measure to the responsiveness to that Spirit by many who came before us. The narrative that follows is offered in thanksgiving to those who have prepared the way.

Early Movements

The first modern-era summons of Christians to united prayer can be seen within a revivalist movement in Scotland in the 1740s. Influenced by the work of Jonathan Edwards, Baptists and various independent churches began to respond to the call to pray together for an outpouring of the Holy Spirit for the revival of the churches. The movement crossed over to America and back, stretching into England and even over to parts of Protestant Europe, sparking energy for Christian outreach and mission. Praying within their own groups, but with common cause and intention, people became deeply aware of the unifying power of such invocation of the Spirit.

The 1840s saw the rise of at least three distinct streams of united prayer. Two of these were calls for prayers for mission. One proponent was a Church of England clergyman, the Rev'd James Haldane Stewart. His tract entitled "Hints for the General Union of Christians for the Outpouring of the Spirit" was published in 1840, circulated widely, including in the United States, and led to high-level meetings between leaders of the Anglican, Congregationalist, Presbyterian and Methodist churches in England. Stewart championed the idea of a day of united prayer on the first Monday of each new year.

English Evangelicals born of the "Awakening" were brought together in 1846 with the formation of the Evangelical Alliance. They carried on the call for united prayer developed by their precursors in the 1740s. Expanding on Stewart's idea of a day of prayer, they called on the members to devote the first week of the new year to a time of prayer by all the membership. The Alliance helped to buoy a sense of the power of united prayer: "The annual celebration of this week of prayer once and for all disposed of the widely-held belief that even evangelical Christians belonging to different Churches could not conscientiously pray together."[1] Other parallel calls for united prayer for mission could soon be heard across the Protestant and Evangelical churches in England, the United States and Canada.

But the first "official" and representatively ecumenical call to prayer for the purpose of praying for Christian unity grew from conversations between the Rev'd Ignatius Spencer, a Roman Catholic convert from Anglicanism, and John Henry Newman, while Newman was still an Anglican. (He converted to Roman Catholicism in 1845.) Newman had previously published a "Plan for Prayer for Union" in 1840, but had not received the necessary support of the Anglican bishops to make it a reality. However, these conversations led to the 1857 establishment, with papal blessing, of the Association for the Promotion of the Unity of Christendom. The key movers of this Association were Anglican Frederick George Lee and Roman Catholics Ambrose Phillips de Lisle and A. W. Pugin. The membership included Roman Catholic, Anglican and Orthodox Christians who committed themselves daily to pray for the visible unity of the Church using the following prayer, along with The Lord's Prayer:

---

1   Ruth Rouse, "Voluntary Movements and the Changing Ecumenical Climate" in Rouse & Neill, p. 321.

O Lord Jesus Christ, who said unto Thine Apostles, Peace I leave with you: My Peace I give unto you; regard not my sins, but the faith of Thy Church; and grant her that Peace and Unity which is agreeable to Thy Will, who livest and reignest for ever and ever. Amen.[2]

Roman Catholic membership was short-lived; the same Pope Pius IX who had given his blessing to the initiative in 1857 condemned it in principle in 1864, and forbade Roman Catholics from entering into such prayer initiatives.

Ten years later, the first Lambeth Conference of Anglican Bishops emphasized prayer for unity in its communiqué. The next year, Lambeth recommended a "season of prayer for the unity of Christendom" over a period of seven days around Ascension.[3] In 1894, the Archbishop of Canterbury dedicated the Octave of Whitsunday (Pentecost) to prayer for the reunion of the churches; this was matched by Pope Leo XIII, who in 1897 called Roman Catholics to a novena (a period of nine days of prayer and devotion) to pray for "reconciliation with our separated brethren" (that those separated would return to Rome). Though proclaimed in perpetuity, it is reported to have been widely followed only after 1908.[4]

The nineteenth century was a turbulent time of political and technological revolutions; cultural changes, from Romanticism to Liberalism; and the growth of cities and of speed of travel and of communication. The churches' responses to this rapid change varied greatly, but the seeds of ecumenism were growing: in part, perhaps, spurred by the increasing complexity of societal, political, cultural and economic life, and the scandal of a broken Christianity that was unable to come fully together in common witness to those societies.

The Rev'd Paul Wattson

Social and religious complexities continued through the turn of the 20th century. Roman Catholics were dealing internally with the conflicts of the Modernist Controversy and its papal condemnation; Protestants had their own internal controversies between Liberalism and the publication of *The Fundamentals* and the emerging Social Gospel movement. Each major Christian tradition, at least in the West, could be said to be challenged by its *own* unity questions as it wrestled with the place of the Gospel and the Church's place in relation to rapidly changing cultures and societal needs during this time.

---

2   Quoted by Ruth Rouse in "Voluntary Movements and the Changing Ecumenical Climate", p. 347.

3   *The Five Lambeth Conferences*. London: 1920, pp. 53, 86, 205, quoted in Rouse, p. 347.

4   See Dagmar Heller, "The Soul of the Ecumenical Movement: the history and significance of the Week of Prayer for Christian Unity," The Ecumenical Review 1998, *Common Understanding and Vision: Continuing the Discussion*. See also Nicholas Jesson, "A short history of the Week of Prayer for Christian Unity" on the website of the Prairie Centre for Ecumenism. (http://www.oecumenisme.ca/pce/). Accessed October 19, 2007.

Paul Wattson was a priest of the Episcopal Church in the United States (Anglican) who was hailed by his contemporaries as the "father" of the Week of Prayer. Amid the turbulence of the world he sought simplicity of life and vision, with a clarity of purpose that eventually came to expression in a vocation as a Franciscan priest and in a theological focus on the centrality of the See of Peter for Christian unity.[5]

Born in 1863, Lewis Thomas Wattson, as he was baptized, was the son of Joseph Wattson, an Episcopalian priest in Maryland. Joseph Wattson had been dismissed from The General Theological Seminary in New York in his student days for overly high Anglo-Catholic leanings, whereupon he had toyed with the idea of presenting himself to the Roman Catholic archbishop of New York. Eventually, however, he returned to Maryland. His Anglican bishop at first encouraged him to "get to Rome, because it is to Rome that you belong,"[6] but Joseph persisted and was ordained in the Episcopal church, where he completed his life's ministry. This bit of personal family history is important. The younger Wattson was raised in a home that was in many ways a typical small-town Anglican rectory, and yet one imbued with a deep sense of connection to the wider Church.

His first published works reflect this connection. In 1894 he founded a small journal called *The Pulpit of the Cross*, which he used for several years as a main venue for sharing his theological reflections on Christian unity and the meaning of "Catholic." At that time he argued that the "church catholic" did not simply mean Roman Catholic. He pushed for a reclamation of the sense of catholic universality within the Anglican communion and beyond, upholding a theory of the "trunk and diverse branches" of the church first articulated by Newman. We need to see our place within the whole "tree," he pleaded. At the same time, to be well rooted in one's faith, one needed (in Episcopal tradition) to submit to the authority of one's bishop. Through the 1890s and until 1909 he considered himself fully Episcopalian and fully Catholic. In fact, he argued that Anglicans were the true Catholics, having continued (in the Anglo-Catholic tradition at least) Roman practices, and not having fallen into "later Latin errors."[7]

The Society of the Atonement

Drawn to the religious life, Wattson spent some time in discernment within the hospitality of the Holy Cross Fathers in Maryland, although he did not intend to become a member of that community. Then, in response to an invitation from Mother Lurana White to serve as interim chaplain to the community of Sisters at Graymoor, he departed for upstate New York, making his home in an austere hermitage at Graymoor. He left the contents of his study behind him, and when not involved in pastoral and priestly work with the Sisters,

---

5   For a detailed biography of Paul Wattson, see Titus Cranny, *Le Père Wattson, apôtre de l'Unité,* 1955.

6   Ibid., p. 11.

7   Ibid., p. 12.

committed himself to prayer. After dedicating three months to the eremitic life (radical solitude), he emerged with a clarity of vision and purpose in his own calling to the vocation of Christian reunion. That vocation, he now knew, needed to be sustained by the work of personal spiritual devotion. On the feast of St. Paul, 1900, he took the name of that saint, and donned the habit of the founder of the Friars of the Atonement. He and Mother Lurana White are credited together as founders of the order and, along with the Rev'd Spencer Jones, of the Week of Prayer for Christian Unity.

The single matter that focused Wattson's theological attention was the question of the earthly *centre* of unity in the Body of Christ. He had experienced what can only be called a conversion to the theology of the primacy of the papacy. It would take him another nine years to act on that theory in practice and become a Roman Catholic, but during those nine years he pleaded, principally with American and English Anglicans, to accept the primacy of the See of Peter. The one error in the English Reformation was that which can be laid entirely at the feet of King Henry VIII, he argued: the break with Rome. In many other things there was honourable reforming spirit, but the split from Rome was akin to a decapitation from which Anglicans have been suffering ever since.

Prayers for Reunion

For several years, early in his vocation with the Friars of the Atonement, Wattson preached widely in the New York state area. Some of these events, which were open-air gatherings in public spaces on Sunday afternoons, felt Franciscan with a revivalist flare. His principal message was that the salvation of Protestantism was to be found in reunion with Rome. The *New York Times* and *Brooklyn Citizen* took notice —of both the crowds he attracted and the controversy (amongst Protestants) of his message. The Anglican response was a typical mix of annoyance, patient listening and the opinion (among some) that the Anglican family is large enough to include such views. But Father Wattson ceased to be a popular speaker in Anglican quarters after his address to a large parish gathering on Long Island. The somewhat "high church" gathering was expecting a presentation of reflections on the spiritual life, but as Wattson entered into a discourse on the challenges of disunity facing Anglicans and began to pronounce on the need for all to return to submit to the authority of the Roman Pontiff, he was cut off by an Archdeacon who began to chant the pre-offertory canticle.

At that point, Wattson retired from public speaking, at least in Anglican quarters. Within the disciplines of his life with the Friars of the Atonement, he offered his communication to the wider world through a series of publications. In the inaugural issue of his journal *The Lamp*, he pleaded that Anglicans minimize the differences that exist between them and Rome, and that the more pressing and larger mission of reunion take its rightful place as the centre. The world's need for a unified Christian witness takes precedence over all other questions, he argued. The emphasis on mission is important. In 1908, he was received for a visit with Cardinal Gibbons, Archbishop of Baltimore, who said to him, "If the Anglicans were with us, we could conquer the world ... You are of good faith, be patient and let yourself be guided by the Holy Spirit."[8]

Later that year, Wattson received a letter from his English (and Anglican) friend Spencer Jones, who suggested that they mount a call for prayer for unity on June 29, the feast of St. Peter. This would be accompanied by prayers and preaching on the theme of Petrine primacy. Wattson welcomed the initiative, which added fuel to his own thoughts of inaugurating an Octave of Prayer for the Unity of the Church. Wattson's idea was to begin on the Feast of the Chair of St. Peter in Rome, January 18, and conclude with the Feast of the Conversion of St. Paul, January 25. The themes were clear: Petrine primacy, the need for conversion to accept that primacy – and the reunion of Christians under Rome for the sake of the mission of the Church. Wattson wrote to Jones that the fruits of such prayer would be seen in the conversion of souls back to the Roman Catholic Church.

The themes of the first Octave of Prayer for the Unity of the Church were as follows:

- 18 January: *Feast of the Chair of Peter of Rome.* Pray for the return of all "the other lambs" into the fold of Peter, in the one flock.

- 19 January: Pray for the return of all Eastern Christians separated from the Apostolic See.

- 20 January: Pray for the submission of Anglicans to the authority of the Vicar of Christ.

- 21 January: Pray that Lutherans and other Protestants of Continental Europe might find the path to return to Rome.

- 22 January: Pray that the Christians of America will return to the See of Peter.

- 23 January: Pray that lapsed Catholics will return to the sacraments.

- 24 January: Pray for the conversion of the Jews.

- 25 January: *Feast of the Conversion of St. Paul.* Pray for the missionary conquest of the whole world to Christ.

The following year, Wattson, along with the entire community of the Franciscan Friars of the Atonement, the Sisters of Graymoor and thirteen lay associates, was received into the Roman Catholic Church in a rare move of corporate acceptance, heralded as the "first fruits of the Great Return." In the same ceremony, Pope Pius X gave his official blessing to the Octave of Prayer. In 1916, Pope Benedict XV encouraged all Roman Catholics the world over to observe the Octave, through the Encyclical Letter *Romanorum Pontificum* (25 February 1916). He went even further, pronouncing a papal indulgence to all who recited the prayers of the Octave.

---

8 Cranny, p. 26.

Revisiting these origins of what we now know as the Week of Prayer for Christian Unity reveals many aspects that can be offensive to non–Roman Catholics. Spencer Jones, Paul Wattson's close friend and a major Anglican supporter of the Octave initiatives, remained a priest of the Church of England. The Week of Prayer tradition was carried into both churches, but only among those who shared views on the necessary submission of all to the Holy See. It would take further developments to shift the Week of Prayer to a more universal ground.

Ecumenism in the 1920s and '30s

Just months after the 1909 papal blessing of Paul Wattson's Week of Prayer initiative, a large representative conference of Protestant and Anglican missionaries was held in Edinburgh, Scotland. Participants in the World Missionary Conference of 1910, many of them highly placed church leaders, began to raise the question of the scandal of division, especially as it led to the exaggeration of competition and division in mission territories. The Great War (1914–1918) only served to amplify the division and the need for God's healing of humanity and of the churches. In the wake of World War I, three streams of organizations that owed their origins to the 1910 Missionary Conference were formed: the Faith and Order movement, to deal with doctrinal questions; the International Missionary Council; and the Life and Work movement, with a concentration on peace and justice issues. These organizations were specifically and strategically aimed to find ways for the churches to work on healing their divisions while working together in mission; we now know them to be the feeder streams of the World Council of Churches, established in 1948.

The eventual achievement of the founding of the World Council of Churches often overshadows the ecumenical story of the 1920s and 1930s. During the period stretching from the economic and technological boom of the Roaring Twenties through the Great Depression and the rise of fascism and conflict, the soul of ecumenism was growing. Father Wattson's Octave of Prayer continued through the 1920s, but other players were gathering on the stage: the Faith and Order movement was gaining momentum; major Orthodox theologians, including Nicholas Berdyaev, began writing about ecumenism; and ecumenical friendships developed. These three other major voices developed their own strength and eventually came into conversation with each other.

Jesus calls us to be friends with one another. The present-day ecumenical movement, whether in local shared ministries, justice and peace work, or international dialogues, knows this well. It is in meeting face to face, learning about God and the world through the other's eyes and ears, coming to share in true friendship that the studying together and the doing together grow into something deeper – something that is truly a sharing in the one Spirit of God. And yet this is the stuff about which it is difficult to write histories.

The "Malines" Conversations

One of the more high profile ecumenical dialogues of the 1920s did not set out to be so – a set of "quiet," unofficial meetings arranged between key Roman Catholic and Anglican theologians in Malines, Belgium, in 1923, often called the "Malines" conversations. Unlike today's official bilateral dialogues, relatively little is known of the content of those conversations. The Archbishop of Canterbury of the time, Dr. Randall Davidson, was quoted as saying that though not sanctioning them, he was following the conversations, which were on core matters of disagreement between the two communions, and hoped that good things would come of them.[9] Anglicans who were not strong Anglo-Catholics, however, were somewhat alarmed. To a casual observer, the major achievement of Malines seems to have been that the meetings happened – that some deep-level theological conversation was able to be pursued for a time and that Cardinal Mercier, Roman Catholic Archbishop of Malines, came to a point, following the conversations, of advocating a great ecumenical council that would work toward the reunion of the churches. Reflecting on the Conversations, Mercier wrote in 1924,

> No book is as valuable as personal intercourse. Conversation sheds light on intimate things which do not pass into print. Men are created to love one another; how often men who are strangers to one another, and who in separation might have felt at enmity, in getting to know one another, experience a moving delight which they had never anticipated.[10]

Quoting an unnamed theologian in the gathering, he added,

> It is probably the first time for four centuries … that scholars, both Protestant and Catholic, have been able to converse, with complete frankness, for hours and hours, on the gravest matters which intellectually divide them, without the cordiality of their relations being disturbed for a moment, or their confidence in the future being shaken.[11]

One of the most lasting impressions from the Malines Conversations is contained within Cardinal Mercier's *Testament*: "In order to be united, it is necessary to love one another; in order to love one another it is necessary to know one another; in order to know one another we must go and meet one another."[12]

---

9 See R.J. Lahey, "The Origins and Approval of the Malines Conversations" in *Church History*, Vol. 43, No. 3 (Sep., 1974), pp. 366–84.

10 See Cardinal Mercier's letter to his clergy, January 18 1924 (Feast of St. Peter's Chair) in *Recollections of Malines* by Walter Frere. London: The Centenary Press, 1935.

11 Ibid.

12 See Geoffrey Curtis, *Paul Couturier and Unity in Christ* (London: SCM Press, 1964), p. 48. Nicholas Jesson comments that "the text was probably written by Dom Lambert Beaudoin.

Viscount Halifax and Father Fernand Portal

Behind the scenes, Malines was the product, at least in part, of an important ecumenical friendship.[13] The Anglican Viscount Halifax and Roman Catholic member of the Vincentian order Fernand Portal had met in 1889 in Madeira, where Portal was chaplain and Halifax caring for an ill child in need of respite from the polluted English air. Their friendship developed out of simple daily routine: living as neighbours, eventually spending long walks discussing matters of religion, and praying together. In and from this friendship, they committed themselves to work for deeper understanding between their churches. Through adversities, such as the declaration of the nullity of Anglican orders in 1896, and Portal's being suspected by his superiors of the sin of modernism, their friendship deepened. The Malines Conversations were the product of the two men's own initiatives of friendship toward Cardinal Mercier. Both Portal and Mercier died in 1926. Just before his death, Portal wrote on friendship and on prayer:

> A friend, a true friend, is the gift of God, even if what we experience together is simply the sweetness of being united in joy and suffering. But if we encounter a soul who harmonises with our highest aspirations, who considers that the ideal of his whole life is to work for the church, that is for Jesus Christ our Master, we become united in our inmost depths. And if it so happens that these two Christians are separated, that they belong to different churches, two different backgrounds, but desire with all their strength and might to knock down the barriers and actively work together to this end, will there be any limits to their power? … The union of the Churches cannot, in fact be achieved except by real apostles, in other words people of faith using spiritual means first of all: prayer which is the source of grace; charity which gives understanding of persons, even those from whom we are separated; humility which leads us to accept our defects and our faults.[14]

The Orthodox Voice

A second important voice is an Orthodox one. Nicholas Berdyaev presented an Orthodox theology of ecumenism that is still strongly relevant today. In a 1927 article, he set out for a non-Orthodox readership the classic distinctions between Western Roman and Protestant

---

Quoted from *L'Oeuvre des moines Bénédictins d'Amay-sur-Meuse*, 2nd ed. (Amay, 1926), translator unknown." See http://www.ecumenism.net/wpcu/history.htm. Accessed October 19, 2007.

13 For a brief overview of the story of Halifax and Portal, see Pat Collins, the online Roman Catholic Charismatic journal "Good News" http://www.ccr.org.uk/goodnews.htm. Accessed October 19, 2007. For fuller treatment, see Cardinal Suenens, "The Ecumenism of Friendship" in *Ecumenism and Charismatic Renewal: Theological and Pastoral Orientations*. 1978.

14 Ibid, quoted in Collins.

traditions and those of Eastern Orthodoxy, and laid the ground of the Orthodox spiritual, mystical understanding of ecumenism. For Berdyaev,

> Ecumenism is not a spatial category and does not need a juristic world organization to express itself. That means: Orthodoxy understands ecumenism more in a spiritual sense. But we Orthodox must admit that the spirit of ecumenism has been so to say only there potentially. [Further] In the Western Christian world, Catholicism and Protestantism are opposite types. But from the point of Eastern Orthodoxy, they appear to belong to the same Western spiritual style. Both have at their center the idea of justification, but not of transfiguration; to both the cosmic conception of Christianity is strange; both have forgotten the Eastern teachers of the Church; and the traditions of Platonism are far remote for them.[15]

Imagine, in the context of how vast the chasm between Protestantism and Catholicism was viewed at the time, hearing that to the Eastern eye, these traditions are two of the same Western type! Orthodox involvement in ecumenical dialogue has made the major contribution of bringing a particular focus and meaning to "spiritual ecumenism." Berdyaev saw in the Protestant approach to Christian unity an opening for involvement of the Orthodox in ways that the Roman Catholic approach of the time did not allow. In emphasizing the unity of Christians, and not working *principally* towards the reunification of one institutional world church within an existing form, he saw a gift. In working to overcome that which truly divides, while allowing for the recognition of a pluriformity of ecclesial expressions and concentrating on the unity of the spiritual body and unity in mission, the Faith and Order movement could be a place where the Orthodox voice could be respected. The heart of real ecumenism is in prayer:

> Reunion and union of the Christian world must begin with community and unification of Christians of all Confessions, with mutual respect and love, with an inner universal spiritual attitude. All must begin with spiritual life, with spiritual unity, and it must work from the inside outwards. Unification of the Churches can only be a work of the Holy Spirit. But we can prepare this work spiritually in our human part, we can create a favourable spiritual soil. Christian unity must not begin with negotiation of Church governances, but with a spiritual unification of Christians, with forming a Christian friendly association, which is possible while also remaining true to one's own creed.[16]

---

15 Ibid., p. 4.

16 Ibid., p. 15.

Robert H. Gardiner

Praying together had laid the foundation for the Faith and Order movement as early as 1919, when Robert H. Gardiner, an American Episcopalian, borrowed from the Roman Catholic Octave of Prayer, which was now officially sanctioned, to create prayer resources as "Suggestions for the Octave of Prayer for Christian Unity." Note the language used of "Christian Unity" and the dates given for the Octave: January 18-25, with, in parentheses, "*January 5-12, Eastern Calendar.*"

Researchers for this anthology were able to locate such pamphlets for 1919–1921 and 1923–1925. The first two, commissioned by the American Episcopal Commission on the World Conference on Faith and Order, were authored and distributed by Robert Gardiner (with his address provided in the inner leaf for ordering information). For the first two years, the January 18–25 dates were retained; however, no mention was made of the feast days of saints Peter and Paul, or any other significance. Beginning in 1921, the dates given were for the eight days, ending with Pentecost/Whitsunday, making similar mention to the dates as they stand in the Eastern calendar.

The early pamphlets were clearly a tool in preparation for the World Conference on Faith and Order, that "with ardent prayer their hearts and the hearts of all their brethren may be given wholly to the fulfillment of our Lord's prayer for their visible unity."[17] They provide a fascinating view into the theology and atmosphere of the times. Entries for each day include brief theological reflections on the meaning of unity, a passage of Scripture, a set of petitions and several collects. A few of the introductory passages deserve presentation in full. This one is from 1919:

> Christian Unity is not negative, but positive; not merely abstaining from ecclesiastical controversies and sectarian competition, but the indisputable evidence which will bring the world to Christ, for it is the manifestation of the one Life of God Incarnate in the Person of His Son that He may offer to man that participation in His Life by which man may be redeemed.
>
> We are too apt to think of unity as if it were merely of organization or government. Christ prayed for a unity of will and love, so that we might have life and power to manifest Him to His world through the Church which is His Body. The motive for unity is the desire to bring the world to Christ, and the only road to success in missions, at home or abroad, the only hope for establishing peace and righteousness and love between nations and classes, individuals and churches, is the manifestation of the one Life, Who alone is able to subdue all things unto himself … If the world is to be convinced that Christ came to redeem mankind, it must be by something that the world can see. So Christian unity must be visible. Spiritual unity alone is not effective,

---

17 From the 1921 Octave of Prayer materials.

for it is not recognized by the world which knows not the things of the spirit. Unity must be spiritual, for the spirit is life, and the spirit of unity is the one Life of the world. But if it be truly spiritual, it will manifest itself visibly.

Spiritual Unity and Visible Unity

Gardiner's work, over these three years, emphasizes the relationship between spiritual unity and visible unity. He reflects on visible unity, in terms of both the reunion of the churches in agreement on core doctrine, and especially the unity that is seen when Christians work together to alleviate suffering and care for the world. Never far from the surface is the reality of the suffering of World War I: the consequences of Christian disunity in its failures to overcome human divisiveness, and the responsibility of Christians to come together in order that the Prince of Peace may bring healing. In Gardiner's words, "The world can no longer endure the horrors that have come upon it; those horrors will increase until we who profess ourselves Christians are willing to be one in Christ that He may be lifted up to do His perfect work."[18] And later, in 1920, "We have seen in the recent war the powerlessness of a divided Christendom to influence the nations and control their passions, ambitions and rivalries. Wealth and social influence or intellectual pride defy the action of the Christian Church broken into separate, if not rival, societies."[19] The vocation of Christian unity was being felt as a matter of salvation, of real and concrete consequence to the life of the world.

As God is diverse and One, said Gardiner, "so in Christian unity the Life of God Incarnate vivifies and binds together and coordinates into the infinity of Himself the diversities of mankind."[20] We have fallen into division by the evils of human will, and so prayer is "not to bend God's will to ours, but to bring our wills into harmony with His, and we can pray only that God will manifest to us the unity He wills and give us grace to follow it."[21] The road is love: "Love is the surrender of self, that self may be found again, transformed, enriched, fulfilled. We do not love one another, and so we do not understand one another and are driven to stand apart."[22] We need each other for our own completion, to correct the errors in ourselves that we don't even know we have until we truly enter into friendship with one another. Mutual love and journeying together reach their fullest expression in the prayer at Christ's own meal. Gardiner ends each pamphlet with prayers and reflections on the scandal of the divided Table. The prayers are offered in a spirit of generosity:

---

18 "Suggestions for the Octave of Prayer for Christian Unity," 1919.

19 "Suggestions for the Octave of Prayer for Christian Unity," 1920.

20 Ibid.

21 Ibid.

22 Ibid.

That if our brethren of other Communions feel bound not to admit us yet to the Sacrament of Unity, we may accept their refusal in humility and love and try to understand that they are compelled by what they believe to be God's will. That if we feel our Communion is bound to refuse that Sacrament to others, we may do it in sorrowing love and with earnest prayer that they and we may come to a fuller knowledge of Him Who is the Truth.[23]

The centre of unity, then, is God in Christ – it is not found in hope for any one organization, or in the upholding of a particular church tradition. Gardiner states,

The manifoldness of God's working in nature, in history, and in His revelation of Himself is to be reflected in the care of His Church for all kinds and classes of men. There should be a large-hearted welcoming of diversities of temperament and thought and custom by the Christian Church, which is to disciple all nations and train all men in the knowledge and love and service of the Son of man, God's Word made flesh.[24]

"Suggestions for an Octave of Prayer for Unity"

The year 1921 marked the first official publication of resources of "Suggestions for an Octave of Prayer for Unity" by the Continuation Committee of the World Conference on Faith and Order, representing Anglican, Armenian, Baptist, Congregational, Czechoslovak, Disciples, Eastern Orthodox, Friends, German Evangelical, Lutheran, Methodist, Moravian, Old Catholic, Presbyterian, Reformed, and South India United churches. The Introduction carries the following call:

The unity of Christendom can be accomplished only by the Church on her knees. Unity in prayer necessitates as well as precedes unity in action. Prayer without action is barren pietism. It must be *united prayer of all* who believe and confess that our Lord Jesus Christ is God and Man … Individual prayer often seems futile. The consciousness of being one of an "innumerable company" praying for the same object at the same time, strengthens one's purpose in prayer. Prayer means immediate and close fellowship with Jesus Christ Who is the Great Intercessor, so that we cease to be lonely in the moment we begin to pray. Moreover, when we pray for Unity we pray for that which He purposes and our prayer is certain of answer.[25]

---

23 Ibid.

24 "Suggestions for the Octave of Prayer for Christian Unity," 1919.

25 "Suggestions for an Octave of Prayer for Unity," Geneva: Continuation Committee of the World Conference on Faith and Order, 1921.

The rhetoric of these pamphlets reaches a particularly vivid expression as the decade moves along. One can hear the Anglican reserve of Gardiner moving aside to make room for a street-preacher voice. From 1923:

> Complacency is a filthy sin; it breaks down the tissues of courage and of consecration till they slough off and are destroyed. It is weak, it is vain, it spends much time before the mirror admiring itself, then goes its way forgetting what manner of character should displace it. It dwarfs the soul; it empties life of the great sincerities; it saps the strength of loyalty, of sacrifice, and of spiritual adventure. It stays at home; it has nothing to share; it is cribbed, cabined, and confined within the conceited and contemptible areas of "his majesty – Myself!" God pity us! His Church is leprous with this disgusting sin. Our separations, which are the very opposition of the spirit of Christ, are exalted, honoured, and perpetuated. The spreading of the glad tidings in the uttermost parts of the world halts and hesitates because of the impotence of the Church complacent in her divisions … How long, O Lord, how long shall variant theology and ecclesiasticism so lord it over God's spiritual heritage, destroying the very foundations of the citadel of love? How long shall our opinions be so majestic and our obedience so errant, our preferences so pompous and our principles so puny?

In 1925, we see a return to the prose of Robert Gardiner. That year, in a testament to the importance of his leadership in the Octave of Prayer movement, Faith and Order reprinted his 1919 text, simply placing the dates for the Octave before Pentecost.

Other than references to its existence and the dates retained around Pentecost, we have little information about the Faith and Order–led Week of Prayer initiatives through the 1930s. Resource pamphlets did not surface in our research about this period. The main story of the 1930s is that of Abbé Paul Couturier and the conversion of the Roman Catholic tradition of the January Octave.

Abbé Paul Couturier

Charles Angell and Robert Mercer, present-day members of the Society of the Atonement at Graymoor, have described the simple history of prayer for Christian unity in this way: "That Christians pray during January for Christian Unity is due to the efforts of Father Paul Wattson of Graymoor. That this prayer is now universal is the realization of the dream of Abbé Couturier."[26]

---

26 Charles Angell and Robert Mercer, "How Christians came to Pray Together." This article is part of the Centenary celebrations of the Week of Prayer for Christian Unity 2008 sponsored by the Graymoor Institute and is found, along with other helpful articles, on their website: http://www.weekofprayer2008.org/centenary-celebration-articles.html. Accessed October 19, 2007.

Paul Couturier was born in Lyon, France, in 1881 to a Roman Catholic family with some Jewish lineage. He was raised mainly in Algeria, but returned to Lyon as a young man. There he found a cosmopolitan city that included a strong population of Protestants among the Roman Catholic majority, and a large number of Russian Orthodox refugees from the Russian Revolution. After his ordination in 1906 into the missionary and teaching order of priests of the Society of St. Irenaeus, he was sent to study science. He served as a teacher until 1946 at the Order's school, a former Carthusian monastery called the Maison des Chartreux.

While still in his 20s, Couturier served the Russian refugee population in Lyon. This was a tremendously formative time for him. About 10,000 refugees had poured into Lyon, and he was at the centre of helping to organize food and shelter and spiritual care. He befriended priests of both Catholic and Eastern rites, learning their spirituality and liturgy and theology while helping to tend to the physical needs of their flocks. This encounter with Orthodoxy left a strong mark on Couturier, forging his vision of spiritual ecumenism. He is remembered as being fond of a saying of one of the Metropolitans of Kiev, that "the walls of separation do not rise as far as heaven."[27]

The Benedictine Influence

The vision of those "walls of separation" falling short of heaven was seared in his mind. It matured during a retreat with the Benedictine Monks of Unity, where he was deeply influenced by the Benedictine tradition of prayer and devotion – not as private undertakings, but at the heart of the whole Church. During his time with the monks, he learned of the Malines Conversations and studied the *Testament* of Cardinal Mercier, whose dictum, quoted earlier, served as a guidepost for Couturier's work. He also met the young Fr. Yves Congar, whose own work would later be very important both to ecumenism and to theological renewal within the Roman Catholic Church. It was through the Benedictines and Congar that Couturier learned of the Octave of Prayer; he took the name Benoît-Irénée in honour of the convergence of these two important spiritual traditions in his own life.

Couturier returned to Lyon from this retreat with the mission of opening his Church's prayer for unity to all Christians, and specifically of reshaping the Octave of Prayer for Christian Unity. As he developed his vision, he insisted that the Week be called "The Universal Week of Prayer for the Unity of Christians." This subtlety reflected his awareness (strongly influenced by Orthodoxy, and by his own personal meditation on John 17 and what he called the "psychology of Christian unity") that unity is ever present and is in need

---

27 Quoted in "The Abbe Paul Couturier and Spiritual Ecumenism," found at http://paulcouturier.faithweb.com, where a good biography of Couturier can also be found. Accessed October 17, 2007. See also the extensive biographical material on Couturier in *The Unity of Christians: The Vision of Paul Couturier – A Special Book Edition of The Messenger of the Catholic League*. October 2003–February 2004, no. 280, edited by Mark Woodruff.

of our discovery. In his view, by praying and finding common holiness together within our different traditions, Christians would discover the gift of Christ's unity. It was more than problematic, to Couturier, to continue a tradition of prayer for Christian unity understood as gathering to pray for all others to return to Rome. There was a deeper centre to which all need to be converted.

The Prayer of Jesus

That centre of it all was the call for all Christians to embrace the prayer of Jesus that we may all be one, as Christ and the Father are one, so that the world may believe. This prayer belongs not to any particular tradition within Christianity, not to any particular church; it is the prayer of Christ himself, and is both beyond and at the heart and root of all churches. In other words, ecumenism does not belong to any one tradition or church: it is Christ's own mandate. Therefore, the spirituality of ecumenism is the spirituality of the whole of Christianity, and it upholds and centres the whole of Christianity. Ecumenism consists of *entering into Christ's own prayer,* according to the will of Christ, and following in Christ's ways. The reality of unity already exists in God's gift and in heaven, away from the plane of history. Lifting ourselves into Christ's own prayer will renew and free Christians together to offer faith to the whole world, for unity among Christians is the sign of the coming unity of all humanity. John 17 is the prototype of all prayer for unity; the Lord's Prayer is the prototype of all Christian prayer. That all Christians could pray the Lord's Prayer together was one of Couturier's greatest dreams.

The Tradition Grows

The year 1933 marked the first public reshaped "Week of Prayer for the Unity of Christians" in Lyon. In fact, it was only three days long,[28] building on the local customs of several religious orders in Lyon that held three-day prayer and reflection vigils beginning on January 18. Each day included a spiritual lecture and special prayers. By 1935, the tradition had grown to a full eight days and, as one local nun remembers, the chapel could no longer hold the crowd. Couturier had arranged for important speakers and made a point, from the very beginning, of extending the invitation to all Christians in the area. The topics of the lectures reflected his conviction that it is in learning about each other, truly encountering each other and growing in mutual understanding, we grow together closer to Christ.

In 1935, for example, the speakers included a prominent Jesuit, Father Perroy, speaking on Ignatian prayer; a Russian Catholic, Father Nedtotchine, speaking about Orthodoxy and the spiritual soul of the Russian people; the famous theologian Henri de Lubac, speaking

---

28 See the colourful description of these early gatherings in Lyon, written by Soeur Marie Madeleine of the Centre Unité Chrétienne in Lyon – available only in French – on their website: www.unitechretienne.org. Accessed October 19, 2007.

about Protestantism; and other speakers explaining the gifts of Anglicanism, the Reformed Tradition and Judaism. It was, at that time, still Roman Catholics speaking about other traditions, but it was a start. The crowds grew and grew, as did participation in the prayers and presentations by non–Roman Catholics. In 1936, the renamed "Week of Universal Prayer of Christians for the Unity of Christians" included a decisive focus on Judaism, which raised the hackles of certain right-wing factions in Lyon that were influenced by what was happening in Germany. That same year, Dom Gregory Dix and several key Anglicans gave lectures, beginning what would become a strong connection between various Anglican religious communities and Lyon.[29] In the same year, 1936, Couturier was invited to organize a series of "spiritual meetings" between Reformed and Roman Catholic leaders in that country. This was the début of what he began to call the "invisible monastery" – a circle of friends from throughout Europe who shared a common vision of spiritual ecumenism. The friendships included the Swiss pastors Roger Schultz and Max Thurian, founders of the (then Calvinist, now ecumenical) community at Taizé; the Sisters of the Reformed Community at Grandchamp, Switzerland; the leaders of the World Council of Churches; and Christians in Sweden and, especially through his friendships with members of religious orders, in England. He made many visits to the Abbey of Notre Dame des Dombes, where he helped to organize dialogues. These were always held within the contemplative prayerful atmosphere that was the hallmark of the community.[30] His work on spiritual ecumenism was a strong precursor to the emphasis on this topic at the Second Vatican Council.

Couturier in Prison

Couturier was imprisoned by the Gestapo during World War II. His many international friendships and visits, and likely his Jewish sympathies, had him branded dangerous. Despite failing health in prison, he managed to keep up a record of correspondence, organize the Week of Prayer, and write many letters giving spiritual sustenance to his friends. Couturier articulated his theology and spirituality of ecumenism in a series of 32 "articles," each several paragraphs long, in a collection entitled *Prayer and Christian Unity*.[31] It was likely written while Couturier was in a Gestapo prison, for its original date is 1944, and it was first circulated only within his immediate community, "for private use." He later published a revised version with the Imprimatur of Cardinal Gelier in 1952.

Prayer and Christian Unity begins with reflections on John 17. The opening words consist of a quotation from Søren Kierkegaard: "True prayer is a struggle with God, in which we

---

29 In fact, Couturier's most important biographer was Father Geoffrey Curtis, of the Anglican Community of the Resurrection in Mirfield, England.

30 Further detail can be found in "The Abbé Paul Couturier, Pioneer of Spiritual Ecumenism" by Sister Teresa Burke, in Woodruff, ed., *The Unity of Christians: The Vision of Paul Couturier*.

31 The full document is published on http://paulcouturier.faithweb.com/pctest01.htm. Accessed October 19, 2007.

are victorious through the victory of God." *Our* work of prayer is to let Christ pray in us to God for unity – to put ourselves into that state of mind, to "have" the mind of Christ who is always interceding for us to the Father. Prayer is a "meeting-place, where, by virtue of charity, the prayers for unity of all true sons of love, all true Christians, even though separated, may flow together into the heart of Christ."[32] One of Couturier's key spiritual insights is an expression of a psychology of spiritual ecumenism: participating in this prayer of Christ pulls us upward to rise above differences. He explains further:

> This "rising above" is by no means negative. It does not imply any dilution or forgetting of our respective beliefs, which are dearer to each other than his own being. This positive action of "rising above" is as true and right for the Protestant, the Anglican and the Orthodox as for the Catholic, in whatever way each is permitted by his beliefs to envisage the problem of Christian Unity. How many situations there are in everyday life where an interior "rising above" is encouraged, even demanded, for psychological well-being. When we are crushed by the death of someone dear to us, must we not force ourselves to "rise above" the memory of the painful separation, to keep faith with the will of the one for whom we mourn, who, being with God, requires of us that we shall be always obedient to the ceaseless calls of the divine will? We must "rise above" what separates us, death – the grave, grief – to find each other again in the unutterable joy of that presence, albeit invisible, of him who has taken one from this world, leaving the other still here for a time … "Rising above," then, is seen to be as it were a psychological law, for realizing, freely and intensely, the interior task we must accomplish. [33]

The Meaning of Conversion

Conversion is the task. However, Couturier was rather cautious in treading this territory, because it had so long been the view of his church that ecumenism meant the conversion of others *to* Roman Catholicism. No: conversion is the ongoing work of the Spirit of Christ in all Christians. Moreover, the conversion that Christ wills is not uniformity nor the sublimation of those differences by which God's love has been made known in the world.

> Each Christian group has its own particular religious riches, and these will be preserved when Christian Unity is restored within the Unity of the Church. This is a fact I would emphasize. "For may there not be, among our separated

---

32 From *Prayer and Christian Unity: Paul Couturier's Testament. In 32 Chapters*. Kierkegaard citation, undocumented, is in Paragraph 1, Chapter 1. This citation from Couturier is from Chapter 4. The Testament is published on http://paulcouturier.faithweb.com/pctest01.htm#The%20 problem%20of%20Christian%20Unity%20if%20not%20'returning'%20but%20're-embodiment. Accessed October 19, 2007.

33 Paul Courturier, *Prayer and Christian Unity*. Ibid., paragraph 4.

brethren, traditional forms of expression, customs, or even doctrinal developments, which are not so easily perceived in the Mother Church?"[34]

He was named "Archimandrite in the Patriarchate of Antioch" and hailed by his archbishop, Cardinal Gerlier, as the Apostle of Christian Unity. When Couturier died in 1953, it is recorded that the Cardinal, breaking one of the major liturgical rules for funeral mass rites for priests, honoured him in a brief, emotional speech before the dismissal.

The Week of Prayer for Christian Unity Gains Momentum

Back in the world of Protestant Christianity, the Week of Prayer tradition remained through the Continuing Committee of the World Conference on Faith and Order. In 1940, Leonard Hodgson, Secretary of that Committee, wrote from wartime England a public letter explaining that the Committee would be considering a change of date for the 1941 Week of Prayer for Christian Unity. For twenty years, Faith and Order had preferred to celebrate the Week at Pentecost. It had long known of the focus and dates of the Roman Catholic Octave of Prayer movement, but had recently been made aware of other organizations, notably the World Evangelical Alliance, that kept dates for prayer for Christian unity in January. Could Faith and Order change its dates to January as well? Doing so would be a reflection of a growing convergence, led in strong part by the movement in France, the work of Couturier, and the growing openness among a number of Roman Catholic theologians who were becoming increasingly attracted to the vision of ecumenism of Lyon.

Having received the affirmation of the Executive Council, the Faith and Order secretariat promoted the 1941 Week of Prayer for the Unity of *Christendom* (italics mine) for January 18 to 25. Full resource pamphlets from that period have not been located, and it seems that the only communication from Faith and Order regarding the Week during wartime was in the form of short letters, and later postcards, from the secretariat, including petitions for prayer. The prayers each year of World War II open with a nod to "the hindrances of the war," during which the work of Faith and Order continued, despite some "challenges," such as the interruption of communication with Holland. In 1941, the secretariat asked for special prayers "that in a world torn by strife and hostility, it is given to us to know that in Christ there is neither Greek nor Jew, circumcision nor uncircumcision, barbarian, Scythian, bond nor free."[35] Communication the next year is brief; the even briefer communication of 1944 is devoted to a celebration of the nearing of theological agreements in the South India proposals, in Episcopalian-Presbyterian conversations, and in Church union negotiations between Presbyterians, Methodists and Congregationalists in New Zealand. The leadership of Faith and Order requested prayers for this continued work in thanksgiving that so much had been able to be achieved despite the difficulties of the times.

---

34 Ibid. Citation is from Jean Guitton, in the *Revue Apologétique*, March 1937, p. 343.

35 From a letter from the Faith and Order Secretariat to member churches of Faith and Order, 1941.

The 1945 Week of Prayer communiqué eagerly looked forward to the gathering of a full World Council Assembly, and outlined the work of Faith and Order as it prepared to become a commission of this World Council that would be established. It asked for prayers for the work to be done on the theology of the Church, ways of worship and intercommunion. Following the end of the war, thanksgiving was made for the reopening of possibilities for international work, and for reunion with ecumenical friends who had been separated by war. By 1946 it was clear that preparations for the world Assembly of the World Council of Churches was well underway. Here is the principal petition for that year's Week of Prayer, as found in the communication from the Secretariat:

> Let us in particular ask for the guidance of the Holy Spirit in the work of our Commissions and in our plans for the future. It will continue to be our part to help the divided Churches frankly to confer together on those questions of faith and order which hinder us from full union and communion, to see that this task and this goal are kept before the minds of the Churches associated in the World Council. May God keep us faithful to this calling and guide us aright as we pursue it.[36]

Faith and Order communications for the Week of Prayer for the remainder of the decade focus on prayer for the leadership of that movement that had become a commission of the World Council of Churches.

After the War

But what was happening outside the central organizational concerns of the Faith and Order Secretariat during these tumultuous years of war and immediate post-war world power realignment? Here is where the stories of lasting impact are to be found – in the experiences of Roman Catholics finding themselves imprisoned and praying side by side with Protestants and Jews; in the necessary cooperation against adversity in the various resistance movements. Willem Adolph Visser 't Hooft puts it well:

> Instead of a period of stagnation, the war proved to be a time of deepening and intensifying ecumenical fellowship. In 1945 Bishop Berggrav could say: "In these last years we have lived more intimately with each other than in times when we could communicate with each other. We prayed together more, we listened together more to the Word of God, our hearts were together more." The struggle to be the Church – essentially one and the same struggle in many countries – the common defence against the ideological attack on the Church Universal, the common suffering, the opportunity to serve prisoners of war and refugees from other nations – these proved more

---

36 From a letter from the Faith and Order Secretariat to member churches of Faith and Order, 1946.

powerful factors in building ecumenical conviction than conferences, committees or journeys.[37]

Visser 't Hooft describes the intimate link between aid and relief given to refugees and prisoners of war during the Second World War, and to refugees after, and the spiritual sustenance and comfort given. Much of this involved close cooperation between the YMCA, YWCA, Red Cross and American Bible Society, along with the Emergency Committee of Christian Organizations, which was founded in the first few months of the war. Another key part of the story of ecumenism during World War II can be discovered in the stories of military chaplains.

Praying for Unity: An Ongoing Activity

It seems a great leap from the postcards of wartime England, with rather truncated Faith and Order committee updates, to the glossy brochures and then full educational, bible study, worship service and prayer resources offered today. That development is due to the increasing cooperation between Roman Catholic agencies and Faith and Order in the production of resources and the promotion of the Week of Prayer for Christian Unity. This cooperation celebrates a 50-year anniversary in 2008, for it was in 1958 that the Centre Unité Chrétienne, the fruit of Couturier's work in Lyon, began working with the Faith and Order Commission of the World Council of Churches. Eighteen years later, following the Second Vatican Council, the Pontifical Council for Promoting Christian Unity (then the Vatican Secretariat for Promoting Christian Unity) entered into the work, making Roman Catholic participation "official" at the highest levels. Since that time, production of the resources for the week has been overseen by a joint committee of these two bodies.

It is fitting that we end this Introduction with words from Paul Couturier:

> Prayer. Is it the fundamental force whose property is to remake Christian unity? Or are other forces needed, equally strong, to forge the healing link? Prayer is the fundamental force. It is fundamental because it is the greatest of cosmic forces; it fertilizes and makes fruitful even the highest of other powers: those of the heart and intellect. These powers are separate gifts, given directly to man by God. But it is only as a result of prayer, whether his own or other people's, that man's powers become fruitful for God. It is man's prayer in Christ, or Christ's prayer in man (which is the same thing), which upholds creation in its due order, gives it harmony, makes it pleasing to God, and makes creation sing, through man, the perpetual praise of thanksgiving to the Creator. Prayer transmutes the world of rocks, plants and animals, into an ordered song: "O bless the Lord, all you works of the Lord." What would the violin and the bow be without the artist who makes them sing? Prayer

---

37 Willem Adolph Visser 't Hooft, "The Genesis of the World Council of Churches," in Rouse and Neill, p. 709.

makes us fellow workers, by grace, with God himself. God, in us, waits for his children to hear "creation groaning and travailing" and when they hear it, they direct it to his glory by the canticle of their prayer.[38]

Bibliography

"The Abbe Paul Couturier and Spiritual Ecumenism," http://paulcouturier.faithweb.com. Accessed October 17, 2007.

Angell, Charles and Robert Mercer, "How Christians Came to Pray Together." http://www.weekofprayer2008.org/centenary-celebration-articles.html. Accessed October 19, 2007.

Best, Thomas and Dagmar Heller, eds. *So We Believe, So We Pray: Towards Koinonia in Worship.* Faith and Order Paper no. 171. Geneva: World Council of Churches, 1995.

Briggs, John, Mercy Amba Oduyoye and George Tsetsis, eds. *A History of the Ecumenical Movement. Volume 3: 1968–2000.* Geneva: World Council of Churches, 2000.

Collins, Pat. "Good News." http://www.ccr.org.uk/goodnews.htm. Accessed October 19, 2007.

Couturier, Paul. *Prayer and Christian Unity: Paul Couturier's Testament. In 32 Chapters.* http://paulcouturier.faithweb.com/pctest01.htm#The%20problem%20of%20Christian%20Unity%20if%20not%20'returning'%20but%20're-embodiment. Accessed October 19, 2007.

———. http://paulcouturier.faithweb.com/pctest01.htm. Accessed October 19, 2007.

Cranny, Titus. *Le Père Wattson, apôtre de l'Unité.* 1955.

Curtis, Geoffrey. *Paul Couturier and Unity in Christ.* London: SCM Press, 1964.

Groupe des Dombes. *For the Conversion of the Churches.* Geneva: World Council of Churches, 1993.

Fey, Harold, ed. *A History of the Ecumenical Movement. Volume 2: 1948–1968, The Ecumenical Advance.* Geneva: World Council of Churches. 1970.

Guitton, Jean. *Revue Apologétique,* March 1937.

---

38 Paul Couturier, *Prayer and Christian Unity*, paragraph 19.

Heller, Dagmar. "The Soul of the Ecumenical Movement: The History and Significance of the Week of Prayer for Christian Unity." *The Ecumenical Review 1998, Common Understanding and Vision: Continuing the Discussion.*

Jesson, Nicholas. "A short history of the Week of Prayer for Christian Unity" on the website of the Prairie Centre for Ecumenism: http://www.oecumenisme.ca/pce/. Accessed October 19, 2007.

Kinnamon, Michael and Brian E. Cope, eds. *The Ecumenical Movement: An Anthology of Key Texts and Voices.* Geneva: World Council of Churches, 1997.

Lahey, R.J. "The Origins and Approval of the Malines Conversations," in *Church History*, Vol. 43, No. 3 (Sept. 1974), pp. 366–84.

L'Oeuvre des moines Bénédictins d'Amay-sur-Meuse, 2nd ed. (Amay, 1926), translator unknown. See http://www.ecumenism.net/wpcu/history.htm. Accessed October 19, 2007.

Mercier, Cardinal. Letter to his clergy, January 18, 1924 (Feast of St. Peter's Chair) in *Recollections of Malines* by Walter Frere. London: The Centenary Press, 1935.

Rouse, Ruth, and Stephen Charles Neill, eds. *A History of the Ecumenical Movement. Volume 1: 1517–1948.* Geneva: World Council of Churches, 1st Edition 1954; 3rd Edition 1986.

Soeur Marie Madeleine, Centre Unité Chrétienne, Lyon: www.unitechretienne.org. Accessed October 19, 2007.

Suenens, Cardinal. "The Ecumenism of Friendship," in *Ecumenism and Charismatic Renewal: Theological and Pastoral Orientations*, 1978.

Woodruff, Mark, ed. *The Unity of Christians: The Vision of Paul Couturier – A Special Book Edition of The Messenger of the Catholic League.* October 2003–February 2004, no. 280.

The First Four Decades

Because it was difficult to track down texts from the earliest years, and there are some gaps remaining, the first four decades (1908–1948) are grouped together.

In these early years, many letters were sent around the world to promote prayer for Christian unity, provide encouragement and keep people up to date on decisions and new approaches. Communication was unpredictable at times, especially during the war years, but people moved forward in hope despite these logistical challenges. Prayers were composed and shared, and the word about the Week of Prayer for Christian Unity began to spread across nations and continents.

Stretch Forth Thy Loving Arms

World Conference on Faith and Order (1919)

He that eateth my flesh, and drinketh my blood, dwelleth in me, and I in him. S. John vi, 56.

The crowning horror and blasphemy of our divisions is that we shut one another out from the one great Sacrament of Love, which Christ instituted as the symbol and means and visible bond of unity, because it is the remembrance of His Sacrifice of Himself for mankind. If the Lord's Supper be only a memorial, yet it is the memorial of supremest love. How dare we join in it, if our hearts be not so filled with love for our brethren that we and they will be constrained to oneness? If it be the approach to the Real Presence of Christ, if it be the reception of His actual Flesh and Blood, if it be the representation of and the participation in the one full, perfect and sufficient sacrifice, oblation and satisfaction for the sins of the whole world, whereby we may receive the very Life of God in Christ, how dare we believe that Christ will deign to dwell in us and we in Him until we are reconciled to Him to the brethren for whom He gave Himself?

God made man free to be His friend or to reject Him. And because we are free, Christ is waiting to complete His redemption of the world till we are willing, by our unity in Him, to manifest Him on the Cross. Shall we continue to let our divisions hinder His perfect work?

So far as by our divisions we hide the Cross, we crucify the Lord afresh, for we keep men from coming to Him to be saved.

Let us pray:

That we may see how far we are individually responsible for the continuance of the divisions which keep from the world the vision of the Cross.

That God the Holy Ghost will help us to search our hearts, if perchance our arrogance and pride of self-opinion have helped to perpetuate and deepen those divisions.

That He may bring us to repent for our aloofness from one another and for all our faults of pride and self-sufficiency.

That if our brethren of other Communions feel bound not to admit us yet to the Sacrament of Unity, we may accept their refusal in humility and love and try to understand that they are compelled by what they believe to be God's Will.

That if we feel that our Communion is bound to refuse that Sacrament to others, we may do it in sorrowing love and with earnest prayer that they and we may come to a fuller knowledge of Him Who is the Truth.

That we may be filled with such true repentance for our guilt that we may be cleansed to reconcile the world to Christ.

Blessed Saviour, who on this day didst hang upon the cross, stretching forth thy loving arms; Grant that all mankind may look unto thee and be saved; through thy mercies and merits, who with the Father and the Holy Ghost art one God, world without end. Amen.

May the God of peace, that brought again from the dead our Lord Jesus, that Great Shepherd of the sheep, through the blood of the everlasting covenant, make us perfect in every good work to do his will, working in us that which is well-pleasing in his sight; through Jesus Christ, to whom be glory for ever and ever. Amen.

Principles for Unity
World Conference on Faith and Order (1921)

The Unity of Christendom can be accomplished only by the Church on her knees. Unity in prayer necessitates as well as precedes unity in action. Prayer without action is barren pietism.

It must be *the united prayer of all* who believe and confess that our Lord Jesus Christ is God and Man – our Saviour and Redeemer. Individual prayer often seems futile. The consciousness of being one of an "innumerable company" praying for the same object at the same time strengthens one's purpose in prayer. Prayer means immediate and close fellowship with Jesus Christ Who is the Great Intercessor, so that we cease to be lonely the moment we begin to pray. Moreover, when we pray for Unity we pray for that which He purposes and our prayer is certain of answer.

Never in our lifetime has there been such a stirring of mankind toward Unity as now. Men are making bold to take definite steps in the direction of Unity. Therefore our prayer must not be for a vague something which we hope may encompass us without any special plan and effort on our part. We must pray for the prospering of those ventures which the spirit of God has put it into our hearts to undertake, and then we can launch out upon them with wisdom and power. "He that hath an ear, let him hear what the Spirit saith unto the Churches."

The Seven Churches of the Apocalypse represent all the Churches in Christendom. Each has its own merits and demerits. But the condition on which it can retain its privileges and rejoice in its glories is repentance for, which involves abandonment of, its sins and deficiencies. It is *Churches* that are called to repentance for their corporate faults as well as individuals for their own shortcomings. No Church can rest in the bland contemplation of its special blessings without jeopardizing its very existence. It can hope to retain its place in God's favor only so far as it recognizes its failures and limitations. Each must set its own house in order for the sake of the well-being of all. And each member of the Church must confess the sins of his own Church as his very own.

Let us then fall to prayer with these principles to guide us.

For the Peace and Unity of the Church
World Conference on Faith and Order (1922)

O Lord Jesus Christ, Who saidst unto Thine Apostles, Peace, I leave with you, My peace, I give unto you; Regard not our sins, but the faith of Thy Church, and grant her that peace and unity which is agreeable to Thy will, Who livest and reignest God forever and ever. Amen.

O God of Peace, Who through Thy Son Jesus Christ didst set forth one Faith for the salvation of mankind; Send Thy grace and heavenly blessing upon all Christian people who are striving to draw nearer to Thee, and to each other, in the Unity of the Spirit and in the bond of peace. Give us penitence for our divisions, wisdom to know Thy Truth, courage to do Thy will, love which shall break down the barriers of pride and prejudice, and an unswerving loyalty to Thy Holy Name. Suffer us not to shrink from any endeavour, which is in accordance with Thy will, for the peace and unity of Thy Church. Give us boldness to seek only Thy glory and the advancement of Thy Kingdom. Unite us all in Thee as Thou, O Father, with Thy Son and the Holy Spirit, art One God, world without end. Amen.

O Lord Jesus Christ, look with pity, we beseech Thee, upon Thy Church weakened and hindered by differences and divisions; bless the effort to bring together in conference all who confess the faith of Thy Holy Name, Who livest and reignest with the Father and the Holy Ghost, God, for ever and ever. Amen.

The Grace of Appreciation of Our Differences
World Conference on Faith and Order (1923)

That the world is very large, that it holds a vast and varied kind of folks, is an almost startling present-day revelation of God.

Races, countries, customs, preferences, experiences, angles of vision and of faith are the colors in the variegated picture of life. The colors to be sure, but not the characteristic, for it is reserved for the unity of the Sons of God to be the real binder, giving all these variant incidentals their divine meaning, significance, opportunity and true realization.

Let us who represent so many different tongues, nations and churches pray for one another that we may possess the grace of appreciation of spiritual gifts however and wherever expressed, and for ourselves that the love of Christ may reveal the common fellowship of all in Him and in His Church, that unitedly we may sing one clear note in divers tones, while unitedly we live in the love and work in the spirit of Jesus Christ our Lord.

The Church of Today

World Conference on Faith and Order (1924)

Let us give thanks for the Church of today; still as ever the mother of Christian character, the home of Christian fellowship, the altar of Christian worship, the scene of an agony in which Christ wrestles for possession of our souls. Let us give thanks for all we can see in the Church today:

of a new spirit of penitence for imperfection in ourselves and our own people;
of a new spirit of charity toward others;
of a new spirit of understanding of their faith and love;
of a new readiness to look with new eyes at old quarrels and disputes;
of a new hunger for truth, and distrust of shibboleths;
of a new recourse to scholarship to illumine the past;
of a new seeking for progress not through controversy but through prayer;
of new efforts toward a purer, more conquering, more transforming life;
of a new faith that effort is worthwhile, since God is God.

For the abiding energy of the Gospel; for the Spirit ever leading us onward into all the truth; for all holy dissatisfaction with the achievement of yesterday, and for an eager striving for a more glorious future, we give thee thanks and praise.

For the present ambition to preach Christ to every nation, and the growing desire to enthrone him Lord over every realm of life, and for the increasing desire to manifest to the world the one life of the Body of Christ, we give thee thanks and praise.

O God the Holy Ghost, Spirit of wisdom and love and power, illuminate and strengthen those who have been appointed to bring about a World Conference on the Faith and Order of thy Church. Give them patience and courage, humility, love and steadfastness, and utter obedience to thy guidance. Fill the hearts of all Christian people with the desire to manifest to the world by their unity its Lord and Saviour Jesus Christ, so that his Kingdom of peace and righteousness and love may be established and all men may be drawn to him, who, with thee and the Father, liveth and reigneth one God for ever. Amen.

Seeking to Be Reconciled

World Conference on Faith and Order (1925)

So long as we look only for errors in our brother, we shall magnify and distort them and harden him in his adherence to them. I may be quite wrong, and you entirely right; yet, as happened often in the black ages when Christians alternated in persecuting each other, you may so assail my error that I will cling to it more closely than to my life, and you may so present your truth that I will gladly be burned at the stake rather than accept it. So you will not only harden me in my error, but you will fall into error yourself, for Christian truth is the manifestation of Christ Who is Love. If I loved my brother whom I think is in error, I might learn of him, for to love is to understand, as to understand is to love.

Let us pray:

That God the Holy Spirit will give us patience to understand those who are separated from us and power to appreciate the truths for which they stand.

That He will show us how to give up whatever is sectarian in our contentions, and how to make plain to our brethren the truth which He has revealed to us.

That God will forgive us for failure to recognize the work of the Holy Spirit among and through our brethren.

That we may have grace to seek to be reconciled to our brethren so that we may be fit to offer ourselves, our souls and bodies, to be a reasonable, holy and living sacrifice unto God.

That we may see that, however our brethren who worship Christ may seem to differ with us, we and they have access by the one Spirit unto the one Father.

That we may have grace to keep the unity of the Spirit in the bond of peace.

When to Celebrate the Cause of Unity

Leonard Hodgson, Secretary, Continuation Committee
World Conference on Faith and Order (1940)

Since 1920 the Faith and Order Movement has kept the week before Whitsunday (Pentecost) as a special time of prayer for the unity of the Church and the work of the Movement. This has been observed by churches and individuals all over the world.

There are other organisations working for unity which have been accustomed to keep January 18th to 25th (the week before the Feast of the Conversion of St. Paul) for this purpose. This began with some members of the Anglican and Roman Catholic Churches; it spread in both these communions in Europe and America; and I have received evidence that the custom of keeping this week in January as a time for prayer for unity is growing in other churches too.

As a result of this, I have been asked whether something could not be done to have an agreed week in which all who care for the cause of unity could join in prayer, instead of having two different weeks observed by different sets of people. I do not think there is any likelihood of those who keep the January week being willing to move into May or June, so that the only way of uniting would be for the Faith and Order Movement to move into January.

I shall have to ask the Executive Committee to consider this matter, but before doing so I wish to discover what would be the attitude to this proposal on the part of the churches and individuals which at the present join in prayer in the week before Pentecost. This year we shall be keeping this week as usual in May. But I am enclosing this letter with the notice of it, and I shall be grateful for any expressions of opinion which will help the Executive Committee to decide what is to be done in future years.

The Hindrances of War

World Conference on Faith and Order (1941)

In spite of the hindrances of the war, our work is still going on.

Statements on the Report of the Edinburgh Conference continue to be received from Churches and we have enough in hand and promised in the near future to make up another pamphlet, which should be issued very shortly.

The most serious interruption has been caused by the breaking off of communications between Great Britain and Holland just after Professor van der Leeuw had been appointed Chairman and Pastor Kooiman Secretary of the Commission on Ways of Worship. But the work of the Commission on the Church is going steadily forward, together with that of the American Co-operating Committee and the American Section of the Commission on Intercommunion. Meanwhile we are collecting material for the use of the European Section of this Commission as soon as it is possible for it to get to work.

Let us remember that in January each one of us will be united with other Christians all over the world who are praying for the unity of Christ's Church and thus for peace and good will among men.

Joining with Heart and Soul in the January Prayers

Leonard Hodgson, Secretary, Continuation Committee
World Conference on Faith and Order (1941)

From 1920 to 1940 the Faith and Order Movement observed the week before Whitsunday (Pentecost) as a special time of prayer for God's blessing on its work. Last year it was decided for the first time to substitute the week between January 18 and 25, thus uniting our prayers with those of many others, both Protestant and Catholic, who are accustomed during that week to pray for the unity of Christendom.

This change was made by the Executive Committee in the light of answers to a letter on the subject which I had received from correspondents all over the world. But owing to the slowness of mails in war time, notice of it did not reach some quarters in time. I am sorry for this and hope it will not happen again.

With regard to the change itself, I should like to say this. My own personal inclination would have been to continue in our old habits. But the observance of the January week was growing, confusion was being caused by people receiving notices of both weeks, from various sides I was being pressed to do something about it, and at last I felt that it would be wrong any longer to prevent the issue being raised by bureaucratic obstructionism on the part of the secretary.

The matter is complicated by the fact that the first week in January is customarily observed by the World Evangelical Alliance as its Universal Week of Prayer, and I have been asked why we did not unite with this week instead of the other. The answer is twofold: (i) our work is specifically work for unity, and (ii) we aim to be inclusive of all Churches, Catholic and Orthodox as well as Protestant. The question of making a change would never have arisen at all if it had not been for the growth of the observance of January 18–25 *for the same purpose and with the same all-inclusive membership* as our own week.

Now that the change has been made, I hope that all who are associated with us will join with heart and soul in the January prayers. The Faith and Order Movement does not exist for itself, but to help the Churches in their own movements towards unity. It is surely right that our prayers for God's blessing on our own work should be set in the context of world-wide intercession for that unity towards which we have to make our particular contribution. In Churches where the week of the Evangelical Alliance has already been observed, it may not be possible to arrange for organised observance of another week only a fortnight later. But I ask everyone who receives this letter to remember that between January 18 and 25 Christians all over the world will be praying for the unity of Christ's Church, and in taking part in that work of intercession to ask for God's continued blessing on the work of the Faith and Order Movement.

Let us pray:

For the healing of the divisions of Christendom, and for that unity which is our Lord's will for His Church.

That Christ our Lord may bind in one those who by many worldly claims are set at variance, and that the world may find peace and unity in Him.

For the blessing of God on the Faith and Order Movement, that it may rightly make its contribution to the cause of Christian unity.

For the guidance of the Holy Spirit for all its officers and committees, and for the chairmen, secretaries, members and contributors of its commissions.

A Common Loyalty to Unity

Leonard Hodgson, Secretary, Continuation Committee
World Conference on Faith and Order (1943)

Let us thank God:

For God's blessing on the American Section of the Commission on Intercommunion; that it has been able to complete its labours and produce its Report.

For all the work that is being done in preparing material for use by the other Commissions when they are able to meet.

That a common loyalty to Christ unites in this work His servants who are otherwise set apart from one another by war.

Let us pray:

For the continued blessing of God on the Faith and Order Movement, that it may rightly make its contribution to the cause of Christian unity.

For the guidance of the Holy Spirit for all its officers and committees, and for the chairmen, secretaries, and members and contributors of its commissions.

That the work now being done by so many contributors may bear rich fruit when the Commissions are able to meet after the war.

Differences in the Field of Faith and Order

Leonard Hodgson, Secretary, Continuation Committee
World Conference on Faith and Order (1944)

Year by year in this week, in every continent, Christians are praying together for the unity of Christ's Church. We in the Faith and Order Movement join in these prayers, praying that the work with which we are entrusted may be blessed and guided so as to help forward the wider cause.

Current events make clear the need of our work. In the discussions on the South India proposals, in the conferences between Episcopalians and Presbyterians in the United States, in the negotiations between Congregationalists, Methodists and Presbyterians in New Zealand – here and elsewhere we see Churches hindered from union by differences in the field of faith and order. We hear them saying that they can get no further without more thoroughgoing theological investigations of the grounds of division.

Let us thank God for the progress that has been made, progress that in many lands has brought many Churches to the point of actually seeking to achieve union.

Let us pray that God's blessing may rest upon all efforts to heal the divisions wrought by differences in faith and order.

Let us pray in particular that through the work of our Movement –

> of the Continuation Committee
> of its Officers and Executive Committee
> of the Commission on the Church
> of the American Theological Committee
> of the Commission on Ways of Worship
> of the Commission on Intercommunion –

the Churches may be helped to find their way to overcome the difficulties which are keeping them from union.

Staying in Touch

Leonard Hodgson, Secretary, Continuation Committee
World Conference on Faith and Order (1945)

In order to reach distant lands by January these cards have to be printed in September. For five years I have had to be content to send them to a narrowing circle of those whom I could reach by post. This September I may surely hope that by January we shall be living in a world in which many of the barriers to communication have been cast down, in which plans for the meeting of the World Council of Churches, which were interrupted in 1939, may again be going forward.

When the Council meets, the Faith and Order Movement will become its Commission on Faith and Order. How does it stand at this moment? And what is likely to be its programme between now and then?

By 1939 the Continuation Committee had agreed that three subjects needed immediate study: (i) the Church, (ii) Ways of Worship, (iii) Intercommunion. On (i) and (iii) American Committees have been able to hold series of meetings, and have produced valuable reports and memoranda for use by our full international Commissions when these can be gathered together. On all three subjects further material has been in preparation for the same purpose. Much of it is in my hands; much, I believe, exists in lands from which I have been cut off, but may reach me by January.

It looks to me as though the next steps will be: (1) the reconstruction of the membership of the three Commissions, (2) the collection and sorting of all existing prepared material and its distribution to the Commissions for circulation among their members. Then (3) each Commission will arrange for the writing of what further papers are needed to fill up the gaps. All this can be done by correspondence. Later on, when this becomes possible, (4) each Commission will arrange for such meetings as will be necessary to produce its Report. It is most important that (3) shall not be concluded, or (4) undertaken until the work can be done on a fully international basis.

This is probably as far as we can look ahead at present.

The End of the War

Leonard Hodgson, Secretary, Continuation Committee
World Conference on Faith and Order (1946)

The end of the war is reopening possibilities of international work. We are at present engaged in seeking news of correspondents from whom we have been cut off for five years, and we hope before long to have our three Commissions on (i) the Church, (ii) Ways of Worship, (iii) Intercommunion established and at work on a fully international basis. The Rev. Oliver S. Tomkins, who has succeeded Dr. William Paton as British Secretary of the World Council of Churches, is assisting me in this work.

We have heard that Professor Van der Leeuw and Pastor Kooiman are both alive and well, but it is doubtful whether their other duties will allow them to continue as chairman and secretary of the Commission on Ways of Worship.

We hope to have a meeting of the Executive Committee at Geneva in February, and to be able then to lay before it detailed plans for the work of the Movement in general and the three Commissions in particular. I shall be grateful for any information or suggestions which may be of use to the Committee. These should reach me not later than February 10th – and the sooner the better.

As we join in the world-wide prayer for the unity of Christendom, let us thank God for the way in which He has kept the work of our Movement alive in lands divided by war, and pray for the guidance of the Holy Spirit as we make our plans for its continuance.

The Future of the Faith and Order Movement

Leonard Hodgson, Secretary, Continuation Committee
World Conference on Faith and Order (1947)

In 1948, when the Assembly of the World Council of Churches meets in Holland, the Faith and Order Movement will be integrated into its structure, our present Continuation Committee becoming the World Council's Faith and Order Commission. At our 1947 meeting we shall have to make plans for whatever adjustments will be required by this development.

As we join with our fellow-Christians who all over the world will be praying for the unity of Christ's Church, let us in particular ask for the guidance of the Holy Spirit in the work of our Commissions and in our plans for the future. It will continue to be our part to help the divided Churches frankly to confer together on those questions of faith and order which hinder us from full union and communion, to see that this task and this goal are kept before the minds of the Churches associated in the World Council. May God keep us faithful to this calling and guide us aright as we pursue it.

A Progress Report

Leonard Hodgson, Secretary, Continuation Committee
World Conference on Faith and Order (1948)

The Continuation Committee met at St. George's School, Clarens, Switzerland, August 28–September 1, 1947 … The Chairmen of the three Commissions reported on the progress of their work; papers were read and discussed: plans were approved for the integration of Faith and Order into the structure of the World Council of Churches next summer.

A full report of the proceedings is being prepared and will be circulated as soon as possible.

Let us thank God

for enabling the Committee to meet again after an interval of eight years;
for the evidence brought before it of valuable work accomplished and in process;
for His guidance in its deliberations, enabling plans to be made for further advance;
for our new Chairman.

Let us pray

For our new Chairman, that God may give him guidance and strength;

For our three Commissions, their chairmen, vice-chairmen, secretaries, members and collaborators, that speaking the truth in love they may be led, and may lead us all, to deeper mutual understanding;

For the World Council of Churches;

For the Provisional Committee in its conduct of its present responsibilities, and its preparations for the Amsterdam Assembly;

For the Churches, appointing their delegates;

For the delegates preparing for their work at Amsterdam;

For God's blessing on the plans for our work in the future, when our Continuation Committee has become the World Council's Commission on Faith and Order.

The World Council of Churches Is Born

Oliver Tomkins, Secretary, Commission on Faith and Order
World Council of Churches (1949)

As in previous years since 1940, Faith and Order uses this week of prayer as an occasion to appeal to all those interested in its work for special prayer, in union with a growing company of Roman Catholic, Orthodox, Anglican and Protestant Christians, for the unity of Christ's Church according to His Will. This year, the appeal comes out of a new setting which is full of promise for the healing of divided Christendom and yet a setting which also reminds us of barriers not yet surmounted and of threats to all that Christians value.

On August 23rd, 1948, the World Council of Churches was constituted. Faith and Order took its place as one of the essential constituents of the new organ.

Let us thank God for having led us thus far and pray for His continued blessing and guidance, especially for the Central Committee and staff of the Council and for the officers of our Commission, and their meetings in July, 1949.

Let us pray that the Commission on Faith and Order of the World Council may be enabled to keep steadily before the Council, in all its aspects, the Divine command to unity in truth and love and may serve the churches participating in the Council even more richly and fruitfully than before.

There were no "observers" from the Roman Catholic Church at Amsterdam, as there had been at Edinburgh and Lausanne, yet there are many evidences of close and sympathetic attention amongst Roman Catholics to the development of the Council.

Let us pray that the Lord of the Church may guide aright those who seek each other across this deepest division of Christendom.

At Amsterdam, the Orthodox Churches of Constantinople and Greece, and the Eastern Churches of Ethiopia and South India, played a full part, but a refusal of any co-operation with the Council "in its present form" was received from the Patriarchate of Moscow and in the name of various other Orthodox Churches.

Let us pray for deeper understanding between Eastern and Western Christians and for the removal of all barriers which prevent free and faithful Christian confrontation between us.

The Amsterdam Assembly met at a time when the horrors of a world war were fresh in our minds and men's hearts fail them for fear of worse to come.

Let us pray that, in such a time as this, God will renew and unite His Church, using the World Council, in all its aspects, to raise up Christians in every land to see their high calling and to walk worthy of their vocation.

The 1950s

Week of Prayer observances of the 1950s – at least in the French- and English-speaking world – followed three distinct movements of prayer for Christian Unity. Each of these was an ongoing and now fairly mature movement in and of itself: Graymoor (in the United States), Centre Unité (in Lyon) and Faith and Order (at the World Council of Churches in Switzerland). Each organization brought a particular emphasis to the understanding of ecumenism, and Christians remained divided despite their prayer for unity. But this was a transitional decade in many ways. The Canadian Council of Churches (founded in 1944), the World Council of Churches (founded in 1948) and other ecumenical agencies were maturing. Creative theological and social forces were at work within Roman Catholicism, preparing the way for Pope John XXIII's initiatives beginning in 1958. Through it all, Abbé Paul Couturier, the prophetic ecumenical personality at Lyon, continued to critique the status quo of all the churches by calling for a deeper conversion into Christ's prayer.

Christians in Canada were living in a society in which the postwar sense of peace and stability was rather short lived, and where social change, through immigration and the massive growth of educational institutions (to give but two examples), was rapid. To counterbalance this insecurity, the popular advertising of the day seems to reveal that huge industries were given over to the promotion of comfort and stability. Canadian neighbourhoods built in the 1950s provided a more cultural (if not economic) mix; yet although Protestant, Anglican, Roman Catholic and Orthodox churches were living side by side, members rarely, if ever, crossed each others' threshholds. Each congregation was content, it seems, in its own corner of the suburb. It was thus courageous to suggest mutual conversation and prayer. But it was even more courageous to call for mutual learning and conversion.

During this decade, the Graymoor community continued faithful to its origins, helping to support the official Roman Catholic celebrations of the Feast of St. Peter's Chair. The materials published in the same year as the Third World Conference on Faith and Order in Lund, Sweden (1952), granting partial and plenary indulgences to followers, remind Roman Catholics that "from the very beginning, the Chair of Unity Octave had no other object than the restoration of all baptized non-Catholics to communion with the Chair of Peter and the extension of missionary enterprises of the Catholic Church throughout the world." An extensive collection of hymns and prayers exalting the Chair of Peter is offered throughout the decade.

Faith and Order, on the other hand, opened the decade repeating Paul Couturier's favourite quotation from the Orthodox tradition: that "the walls of our division do not reach to heaven." Institutional concerns, in these early days of the WCC, are balanced with care for the world. There is much to pray for and to celebrate within the World Council of Churches' work and in the world. Prayers were offered for the Lund and Evanston meetings,[39] and for the theological commissions that were helping the churches to deepen their understanding of what each meant by "the church." A deep awareness of the separation of Christians by the solidifying Iron Curtain was also brought to prayer.

In Canada, the Canadian Council of Churches established its own Faith and Order Commission in 1950 to help keep theological and spiritual matters at the heart of ecumenism, and to maintain links between Canadians and the worldwide ecumenical work.

The prophetic sibling, the Centre Unité in Lyon, went even further. Each year's materials opened with the simple observation of how many people there were in the world, how many Christians, and how many different churches: how the world is waiting for the children of God to be revealed *together* as one body. Jesus unites us and we are all gathered under his cross. The cross is the way of salvation that we share, and the journey of repentance to which we are all called. What was prophetic about this voice was that it called *all* churches to conversion through confronting the sin of separation and walking a road of repentance. Litanies offered particular petitions – for the ways in which we have failed to listen to each other, failed to care for each other, failed to love each other, turned to violence against each other. We call each other to turn to the Bible and to Jesus and to reach out in humility and genuine self-giving to the other. For how can we love that which we do not know?

In Canada, the Canadian Council of Churches' Department of Evangelism picked up and elaborated on the Faith and Order materials, while the Montreal Centre for Ecumenism distributed the Lyon materials. As time went on, these two bodies would cooperate more intimately in the Week of Prayer for Christian Unity.

J.E. Scully

---

39 Second Assembly of the World Council of Churches, Northwestern University, Evanston, Illinois, USA, 1954.

Preparing for the Third World Conference on Faith and Order

Oliver Tomkins, Secretary, Commission on Faith and Order
World Council of Churches (1950)

Once more Faith and Order invites all who care for its work to join in prayer for the unity of the Church of Jesus Christ according to His will. This week of Prayer for Christian Unity becomes increasingly a time when Roman Catholic and Protestant, Anglican and Orthodox Christians recognize in thankful intercession that "the walls of our division do not reach to heaven." The Faith and Order Commission of the World Council of Churches calls you to join in this universal prayer with certain particular petitions in mind, because the Commission exists in order to be the handmaid of the Churches as they themselves face Our Lord in His eternal prayer for our unity.

So *let us pray* especially for the plans being made by the Commission for a third world conference on Faith and Order to be held, God willing, at Lund in 1952, that the conference and the preparations for it may lead all the participating churches to deeper perception of the Truth Whom they serve.

Let us pray for the three Theological Commissions which have for some years been preparing material for the Conference: that the first may deepen mutual understanding of what each means by "*the Church*" and lead us all nearer to accepting what God means by the Church;

> that the second may illuminate for all the varied traditions in *Ways of Worship* and serve the offering to God through Christ of that praise which is our bounden duty;

> that the third may give the light which we need on the question of *Intercommunion*, because the Sacrament of Unity has become an occasion of division.

Let us pray for the more honest and courageous recognition of those forces in history, political, economic, cultural, which have influenced our divisions, and for grace to recognize, under the Lord of history, similar forces which may assist our recovery of unity in Him.

Let us pray for all those who take no official part in the preparations for Lund, but follow our work with sympathy and prayer; especially thanking God for ecumenical spirits in the Church of Rome. Let us pray too for those Christians, Orthodox and Protestant, in U.S.S.R., in Eastern Europe and parts of Asia, who are debarred from personal participation, especially for all who, under restraint or persecution, cannot express the unity they have with us in Christ.

For the Reconciliation of Differences

Oliver Tomkins, Secretary, Commission on Faith and Order
World Council of Churches (1951)

Once more we join the Christians of many confessions to invite you, as you pray for the unity of the Church of Christ according to His will, to pray also for the work of 'Faith and Order.' From other sources, we hope, you will be receiving suggestions on prayer for unity during this Week, since its observance is slowly but surely gaining ground in many countries. Either in your personal prayers or as you lead corporate prayer, will you remember some of the following concerns which occupy our minds in 'Faith and Order' as we prepare for the conference to be held, God willing, at Lund in 1952.

The Nature of the Church: let us pray for ever deepening understanding of the nature of the Church in the purpose of God;

> for all biblical scholars and theologians whose work is revealing unexpected new sympathies and areas of agreement as they seek to get behind the misunderstandings created in recent centuries;

> for all whose faithful witness to the truth as they have received it enlarges the understanding of those from other traditions;

> for patience and faith to overcome apparently impenetrable barriers to agreement, sustained by the belief that, since our Lord wills unity, He can bring us to it.

Ways of Worship: let us pray for those in all churches who are discovering afresh the riches inherent in the great tradition of Christian worship, especially the ever-fresh meaning of that Sacrament which our Lord instituted at His Last Supper;

> for all ways in which the common inheritance of worshipping Christians may lead to the reconciliation of differences which have grown up between us;

> for such a sharing of experience in prayer and worship that the inner meaning of our beliefs may become plain to those who have grown up in another tradition;

> for such a deepened understanding of the Spirit and the truth that we may be drawn closer to the Father who would have us to worship Him.

Intercommunion: let us pray for a more widespread and urgent awareness of our separation from one another at the Lord's Table;

> for a better appreciation of the convictions held in this matter by those with whom we disagree and the ability to believe in each other's integrity;

for all those, especially young men and women and members in the Younger Churches, who find our divisions to be incomprehensible, and so our barriers to communion to be quite intolerable;

for the removal of all hindrances to a true communion with one another, in truth and love, in the Sacrament of Unity.

Other Matters: *let us pray* for an honest understanding and admission of those various political, economic, social and other factors which helped to cause or perpetuate our divisions;

for the ability to recognize and accept the pressure of similar factors in our own time which, by God's grace, may lead us to unity if we have no real theological reasons for continued separation;

for all who are engaged in actual schemes or negotiations for unity, that they may be led into unity in the truth and that their zeal may be an encouragement to others;

for God's blessing upon the meeting of the Faith and Order Commission (August 14-18, 1951) which will have to complete plans for the Conference at Lund to which the churches have been invited to send delegates.

A Great Hope

Abbé Paul Couturier (1952)

At long last, Catholics are coming back to the Bible. It is a homecoming that fills the hearts of our Protestant brothers and sisters with tremendous joy. And rightly so. Once again, we are beginning to understand the words of St. Jerome, found in his Prologue to Isaiah: "To be ignorant of the Scriptures is to be ignorant of Christ." This return to the Scriptures will have two far-reaching consequences.

Here is the first. When Catholics have relearned how to read, study, and above all reflect on the Word of God, and when they have done so with all the necessary prudence and under the guidance of the Church – who has preserved this divine treasure for them and now presents it to them – they will discover that they share with their Protestant and Anglican brothers and sisters a common foundation. Their unconscious and their subconscious will be immersed in the same life-giving spirit. They will grow much closer to their non-Catholic Christian brothers and sisters in their ways of feeling, judging and thinking and in their spirituality. We will finally be able to understand one another.

The second consequence of our return to the scriptures is this. Just as the Divine Mind, the Word of God made flesh, Christ … is set before us – in time and space – through creation (of which the Divine Mind is, moreover, itself the cause), so the history of that gradual process of creation is set before us in the Scriptures, filled with the Mystery of Christ, by whom and for whom all things were made. To grasp the meaning of this Mystery of Christ in the Scriptures is a divine task that can only be accomplished in us, in all Christians, by the Spirit of Christ, the Holy Spirit. Thus we are faced once again with the great necessity of prayer.

The higher an airplane rises above the ocean – up to a certain altitude – the more clearly it can distinguish how deep the ocean is. In the same way, when we apply ourselves in prayerful and reflective study, the higher our level of spiritual maturity, the more clearly we shall be able to see, hidden in the deeper meaning of the Scriptures, how beautiful is the mystery of Christ.

In His Mystery, we will gradually discover the other mysteries, the mysteries of such privileged human beings as the Virgin Mary, John the Baptist, the Apostles (Peter, Paul, John …), Joseph the husband of Mary … Does not even the simplest creature have its hidden mystery in the Mystery of Christ?

Under the express condition of a spiritual maturity sustained by fervent prayer, theologians who have become biblical scholars and biblical scholars who have become theologians will, in their common search to understand the mystery of the same Christ, be able to discover that Christ and His Church are one.

Then the seemingly most insignificant details, signs and clues in the Scriptures will be discovered as shedding light on the hidden destiny in Christ of certain persons, for example, the Virgin Mary. And from just these minute details, we will be able, all of us together, to enter into that person's destiny and understand it in the same way, in its own reality. For this to happen, the great scholars, Catholic and Protestant alike, will have to become "meek and humble of heart," for it is to "the meek and the humble" that mysteries are revealed. This great hope needs to be nurtured by all Christians through their intercessory prayer, failing which it would lose its vitality and never produce the rich fruit of Unity – its hidden treasure.

We must love the Bible. We must read, ponder, and pray the Bible. The Bible is a "formidable" book, but so are all the great sources of spiritual energy. That is to say that reading it demands prudence, guidance and initiation. Catholics now have access not only to the Bible, but also to the books and other means that will help them know how to read it and draw sustenance from it … All this, available at all levels of society.

The Work of Faith and Order

(World Council of Churches, 1952)

Once more we join with Christians of many confessions in prayer for the unity of the Church of Christ according to His Will. From other sources, we hope, you will be receiving suggestions on prayer for unity during this Week, since its observance is slowly but surely gaining ground in many countries. But, as we pray in general for the unity of the Church, so we invite you to pray in particular for the work of Faith and Order as it seeks to serve the end of unity. Either in your personal prayers or as you lead corporate prayer, will you remember some of the following concerns which occupy our minds in 'Faith and Order' as we prepare for the conference to be held, God willing, at Lund from August 15th to 29th, 1952.

Let us pray:

- for the Churches which will be represented at Lund: that their delegates may be wisely chosen and fully prepared for giving a true impression of their own traditions and for receiving sympathetically the testimony of others:

- that behind the delegates there may be in all churches a large body of informed opinion and sincere prayer:

- that all churches may be delivered from merely human motives of self-justification and self-assertion and be sensitive to the demands of God's truth and love.

Let us pray:

- for the churches which will not be represented at Lund: that churches, cut off from their Christian neighbours by the suspicion and mistrust engendered in our divided world, may not lose their awareness of unity in Christ which transcends all political and ideological divisions:

- that churches in Communist-dominated countries may know such a deepening of Christian faith and life that they may draw nearer to the Centre of our unity even whilst our human contacts with each other are weakened or destroyed:

- that the Church of Rome may truly understand the purpose of our ecumenical fellowship with each other even whilst she cannot see her way corporately to take part in it:

- that all Christians who suspect or denounce our fellowship may be led only by a zeal for truth and may act with charity.

Let us pray:

- for those who are responsible for the organising of the Lund Conference:

- that the reports and volumes of the Theological Commissions may be used by God for the dispelling of ignorance, the disarming of suspicion and for the building up of the Body in love:

- that the worship at the Conference may be so planned and so led that our differing traditions become the means not to deepening confusion but to deeper awareness of the Spirit and the truth:

- that the Lund Conference may result in 'Faith and Order' discovering afresh how to serve the churches in overcoming their divisions and manifesting the essential oneness of the Church of Jesus Christ, until such time as our work is done and God is pleased to establish in its fulness the unity He has given to us in His Son.

A Prayer

O Lord Jesus Christ, Who didst say to thine Apostles, Peace I leave with you, my peace I give unto you,

Regard not our sins but the faith of thy Church

And grant unto her that peace and unity which are agreeable unto Thy Will,

Who, with the Father and the Holy Ghost, livest and reignest for ever one God.

Amen.

News from the World Council of Churches

Oliver Tomkins, Secretary, Commission on Faith and Order
World Council of Churches (1952)

Dear Friend,

As we have got into the custom of doing, I am sending to all you whose names have over the years come to compose the Faith and Order mailing list this letter to accompany the notice reminding you of the Week of Prayer for Christian Unity, which has been observed in the Faith and Order movement since 1942.

I am afraid it is not possible to present everybody with the report of the Faith and Order Conference at Lund, but you may be interested to know the following particulars about how it may be obtained:

(a) From S.C.M. Press Ltd., 56, Bloomsbury Street, London, W.C.I., at 3s 6d.

(b) From World Council of Churches, 156, Fifth Avenue, New York 10, N.Y., U.S.A., at about 40 cents.

(c) From Oekumenische Centrale, Frankfurt a.M., Schaumainkai 23, Germany (in German).

(d) From Conseil Œcuménique, 17 route de Malagnou, Geneva, Switzerland (in French, available shortly).

As in the case of the Lausanne and Edinburgh Conferences, we hope to produce a large volume reporting the Conference proceedings in detail. At present arrangements have only been made to bring out an English edition, through the S.C.M. Press, London, but the possibility of German and French editions is under discussion. Full details will be announced to the churches as soon as they are known, and doubtless you will see news of the publication as soon as it is ready. Meanwhile, at the end of the small Faith and Order Report a list of all the other available Faith and Order publications is given.

You have probably read somewhere or other about the Lund Conference. In some countries the religious and secular press gave it careful and sympathetic attention. In other cases it was reported with a good deal of misunderstanding and ignorance, unfortunately sometimes tinctured with ill will. But the main thing is that the Report is now before the churches for their judgment, and the new Faith and Order Commission has been appointed with an embarrassingly rich series of suggestions from the Conference as to work in which Faith and Order might be engaged. We were happy that Archbishop Brilioth consented to remain Chairman of the Faith and Order Commission (which will probably hold a meeting adjacent to the Evanston Assembly in 1954, but will normally meet every three years). As most of you know, I have resigned my post as Secretary, in the conviction that the time has come, after eight years of work as an ecumenical secretary, when I could serve the ecumenical cause better from a base within the life of my own church. I have been called to become Principal of a Church of England theological college in the cathedral city of Lincoln, but I am happy to keep contact with Faith and Order through having been invited to become Chairman of its Working Committee. So I hope to be able to continue directly in touch with Faith and Order, as well as being able to commend the ecumenical movement to those who are preparing for the ministry.

My successor is Dr. J. Robert Nelson, of the American Methodist Church, whose book *The Realm of Redemption: Studies in the Doctrine of the Church in Contemporary Protestant Theology* was written whilst studying under Dr. Brunner at Zürich. It has been very well received, and indicates something of the qualifications which he brings to the work. I am sure he will value, as I have done, every opportunity of contact with the many friends of Faith and Order on the mailing list, and that he will do his best to keep in touch with you.

On behalf of the Commission, I send you Christian greetings, within the fellowship of desire to which we belong together.

Our Own Sins

Centre Unité Chrétienne, Lyon (1953)

"If we do not acknowledge all of that [the sins of the clergy and the faithful], then it is in vain that we come together in Council, in vain that we call upon the Holy Spirit, who first enters the soul of a person when that person has been found guilty - in order to 'prove the world wrong about sin' (John 16:8). Until we ourselves have experienced the Holy Spirit's condemnation of us, we cannot say that we are filled with the Holy Spirit, and the Holy Spirit will not enter our souls if we refuse to be mindful of our own sins…."

(Admonition of the Papal Legates at the Second Session of the Council of Trent, January 7, 1546.)

For a More Perfect Dedication to God's Will

World Council of Churches (1953)

Let us pray – that the unity which it has been given to the churches to experience together may now find clearer manifestation:

- that our churches may earnestly consider whether they are doing all they ought to do to manifest the oneness of the people of God.

Let us pray – that a more profound study together of the doctrine of the person and work of Christ and of the Holy Spirit may lead to deeper agreement upon the doctrine of the Church:

- that we may know more truly that the way of Christ is the way of the Church and that the mystery of His life is the mystery of the Church's life.

Let us pray – for growth of agreement upon the nature of the Church's unity and continuity as the visible fellowship in which all members, acknowledging Jesus Christ as living Lord and Saviour, shall recognize each other as belonging fully to His Body, to the end that the world may believe.

Let us pray – that all Christian people may cultivate a sympathetic and reverent attitude to all the forms of worship in which God confronts man:

– that so they may be led to reflect upon the question of how far varieties in worship within our different communions make it possible to conceive of a similar rich diversity within a united Church.

Let us pray – that discussion of the painful problems surrounding intercommunion may be made more fruitful and more charitable by the acceptance of clear and agreed terms in which to discuss it:

– that both those who advocate and those who oppose intercommunion before full union may respect each others' convictions and that both may strive for the resolving of their differences.

Let us pray – for a more perfect dedication to God's will, so that all Christians, returning humbly to the only springs of mercy and power, may find that their feet are set firmly upon the path to that unity which God has designed for His people.

The Heart of Christian Unity

Centre Unité Chrétienne, Lyon (1954)

As *all* Christians are, more or less, responsible for the current fragmented state of Christianity, they must all participate in repairing the damage. Christians must make reparation before God, who has been publicly offended, before humankind, which has rightly been scandalized, and before all of creation, visible and invisible (as creation has a mysterious and real relationship with Christians, who are vitally bound to Christ, and as creation's journey towards "Christification" has been slowed under the weight of a fractured Christianity). They must do so together, at the same time, and in a visible way, insofar as that is possible. This simultaneousness will bring with it the benefit of not just added spiritual strength, but multiplied spiritual strength in reparation and intercession. It is because the disciples are together (and in this case, they will be together to the extent that they are able), that Christ is in their midst. This simultaneousness will contrast with the ugliness of their fragmentation, and finally allow Christians to *offer* to their non-Christian brothers and sisters, and to all of expectant creation, the moving and visible beauty of the Unity of their spiritual efforts, the prelude and promise of Christian Unity, transcending any beauty arising from the harmonizing of purely human efforts …

One could examine any other problem standing in the way of progress along the path to Christian Unity, and we would still reach the same conclusion: "The question of Christian Unity, for all of us, revolves around our inner disposition." For if our inner life were not disposed to Christian Unity, even in private, how could this burning issue take hold of

Christians? And if it did not manage to captivate, even *torture*, the Christian conscience, then really, how could it ever be resolved?

Unite Us in Truth

World Council of Churches (1954)

Leader: Almighty God, who didst make with us the New Covenant and said,
I will be their God and they shall be my people,

All: *Forgive and heal our divisions.*

L: Merciful God, who didst name Thy Son Jesus,
that He should save His people from their sins,

All: *Forgive and heal our divisions.*

L: Lord Jesus Christ, who didst promise that where two or three
are gathered in Thy name, Thou art in their midst,

All: *Unite us in Thy truth.*

L: Son of the Living God, who didst assure Thine apostle
that the gates of hell shall not prevail against Thy Church,

All: *Unite us in Thy truth.*

L: Good Shepherd, who wilt gather all Thy chosen sheep in one fold,
so there will be one flock,

All: *Unite us in Thy truth.*

L: Lamb of God, who didst give Thyself for the Church
and make it one Body in the Baptism of the one Spirit,

All: *Unite us in Thy truth.*

L: Bread of Life, who didst give the one Loaf and the one Cup
for the nourishment of the Church which is Thy Body,

All: *Unite us in Thy truth.*

L: Spirit of God, who dost bestow diversities of gifts upon Thy people
for the edification of all,

All: *Maintain our unity in the bond of peace.*

L: Holy Spirit, who dost help our weakness of prayer and make intercession for us,

All: *Maintain our unity in the bond of peace.*

L: Father, Son, and Holy Spirit, one God everlasting, forgive and heal our divisions,
unite us in Thy truth, maintain our unity in the bond of peace.

All: *Amen.*

Prayer of St. Dionysius
World Council of Churches (1955)

O God, the Father, in whom is calmness, peace and concord; make up the dissensions which divide us from each other, and bring us back into a unity of love, which may bear some likeness to Thy divine nature. And as Thou art above all things make us one by the unanimity of a good mind, that through the embrace of charity and the bonds of affection, we may be one, as well in ourselves as in each other; through the grace, mercy and tenderness of Thy Son, Jesus Christ. Amen. (*adapted*)

An Enduring Indifference
Centre Unité Chrétienne, Lyon (1955)

Nine centuries have passed since the greater part of the Christian East separated from Rome.

More than four hundred years have gone since the Reformation.

… And the bulk of hundreds of millions of Roman Catholics, Protestants, Orthodoxes and Anglicans live, to say the least, in a kind of indifference towards one another.

If you were asked: "What is a Protestant? – or a Roman Catholic? – or an Orthodox? – or an Anglican?" … you would most probably be inclined to point out to whatever displeased you, or, at any rate, was a root of dissension.

You do not know them!

How then can you value and love them?

Hear Us and Save Us, Good Lord

World Council of Churches (1956)

Leader: Almighty Creator and Redeemer of all men, who didst graciously choose, call and covenant with Thine own People, we adore Thee for Thy deep wisdom and unsearchable judgements.

All: *Praise be unto Thee, O Lord.*

L: Eternal God, who didst send Thy Son Jesus Christ as the promised Messiah and Saviour of Thy People, we rejoice and thank Thee for Thy steadfast love.

All: *Praise be unto Thee, O Lord.*

L: O Son of Man and Suffering Servant, by whose atoning death we have been made one with Thee and with each other, grant us contrition and penitence for our continued divisions, which obscure the sufficiency of Thy sacrifice.

All: *Hear us and save us, good Lord.*

L: Good Shepherd of our souls, who has lived and died to gather into one the scattered children of God, take from us all such waywardness and willfulness as continually disperse and estrange Thy flock.

All: *Hear us and save us, good Lord.*

L: Thou who art the true Vine, of which we are all branches, so abide in us that we may abide in Thee, and by Thy Word so cleanse us of hostility and pride that we may bear much fruit for Thy glory.

All: *Hear us and save us, good Lord.*

L: Thou loving Bridegroom of the Church, who has cleansed and consecrated her to be presented holy and unblemished in the day of Thy coming, purify us her members from the ignorance and sloth which divide us in our witness and service.

All: *Hear us and save us, good Lord.*

L: O sacred Head of Thy Body, the Church, grant us grace both to maintain the unity of the Spirit and to attain to the unity of the faith in knowledge of Thee, that we may follow after peace and mutual upbuilding.

All: *Hear us and save us, good Lord.*

L: Holy Spirit of God, in whose communion we have life, and by whose gifts we are strengthened, lead us despite our divided state into the truth of Christ and empower us to do all things needful to show forth the unity of the Church.

All: *Hear us, save us, heal and unite us, good Lord. Amen.*

Gather Thy Church, O Lord

World Council of Churches (1957)

Leader: As this bread was once scattered upon the mountains, and has now been gathered into one, so may Thy Church be gathered into the unity of Thy Kingdom: All glory be unto Thee, O Lord, for ever and ever!

Response: Gather Thy Church, O Lord, from the four winds, into the kingdom of Thy Love.

L: Holy Father, we thank Thee for Thy Holy Name, which Thou hast imprinted upon our hearts, and for the knowledge of faith and immortality which Thou hast brought to light through Jesus, Thy Servant.

R. Gather Thy Church, O Lord, from the four winds, into the kingdom of Thy Love.

L: Have mercy, O Lord, upon Thy Church,
Deliver her from all evil,
And perfect her in Thy Love.
Gather her out of the nations
Into that unity which Thou hast prepared,
And unto Thee be the Power and the Glory,
for ever and ever!

R. Gather Thy Church, O Lord, from the four winds, into the kingdom of Thy Love.

L: Come, Lord Jesus, come!
Glory be to thee for ever and ever. Amen.

R. Gather Thy Church, O Lord, from the four winds, into the kingdom of Thy Love.

The Lord's prayer …

A Kingdom for All

Centre Unité Chrétienne, Lyon (1957)

Lord Jesus Christ,
you were born of a Jewish mother,
but you rejoiced greatly
in the faith shown by a Syrian woman and a Roman soldier;
you welcomed with kindness the Greeks who sought you,
and you let an African man carry your cross.

Grant us also that we may welcome people of every race
into your kingdom as co-heirs.

The Fruit of Victory

Centre Unité Chrétienne, Lyon (1958)

To love our brothers and sisters is a source of suffering:

- – for we will see even more clearly what the real issues that separate us are;

- – for we will grasp with greater lucidity that it is in the name of our deep loyalty, to Jesus Christ and to our faith, that we became separated;

Because we love, our desire to be together, in total Unity, will only be more ardent. This desire will then be purified by the Holy Spirit, the Spirit of Love.

We will understand even better all that needs to be purified in us, so that our Unified prayer may fully bear fruit.

And, since "love never rests," we will never say that we have done enough or that we are satisfied, when the Word of God seeks to penetrate our hearts more deeply.

Christian Unity will necessarily be the fruit of a victory over the pride and selfishness of each one of us. That is why bringing about Christian Unity is a slow process. We will only be one when all egotism has been removed from us. (Father Voillaume)

"Where charity and love are, there is God." (Holy Thursday Liturgy)

"Let us love one another so that in the unity of the spirit, we may confess the Father, the Son, and the Holy Spirit, the consubstantial and indivisible Trinity." (Liturgy of St. John Chrysostom)

Praying Aright

Oliver Tomkins, Chairman, Working Committee of Faith and Order
World Council of Churches (1959)

In sending out once more these suggestions for the observance of the Week of Prayer for Christian Unity, the Faith and Order Department of the World Council of Churches expresses its desire to see this particular period become the focus point of continual and widespread prayer for unity. But comments which have reached the Faith and Order Committee suggest that two points should be made now, which may perhaps remove some uncertainties.

1. Confusion exists in some quarters between this Week of January 18th to 25th and a Week of Prayer earlier in January, promoted in many countries by the World's Evangelical Alliance. Enough to say that the two observances have widely different origins and purposes, but need not conflict in spirit or practice. The Evangelical Alliance is concerned with united prayer for the evangelization of the world. "Our Week" is concerned with prayer for unity. Unity and mission are so closely related that we ought to find no conflict in the spirit of the two weeks, though it must be admitted that this nearness does, in some quarters, create real problems of a practical and organizational kind. But these have to be sorted out at the local level.

2. Another confusion is between the observance of this Week in the spirit and approach associated with the name of the Abbé Couturier (whose outlook was one which the Faith and Order movement shared when it adopted the promotion of this Week in 1940) and an interpretation of it as prayer simply for the reconciliation of all the other Christians to the Roman Catholic Church. Of course, every Christian must have *some* conception of what he believes would be involved in our prayer for unity being answered. We know that there are many Christians who observe and advocate the Week of Prayer in the belief that it must be thus interpreted. But this knowledge need not for one moment hinder us from commending an observance of the Week which leaves the definition of it, in human words, "that the visible unity of the Church of Christ may be accomplished according to His will and by the means that He wills."

That is the prayer which we would commend to all, as a prayer that may be made in complete sincerity and honesty, and in the faith that "the walls of our division do not reach up to heaven."

May the Holy Spirit of God teach us all to pray aright.

A Heart Capable of Loving

Centre Unité Chrétienne, Lyon (1959)

O God of love,
You who, through your beloved Son,
gave us the new commandment to love one another
with the same love with which You Yourself loved us,
poor, unworthy and lost;
with the same love which moved you
to the point of giving us your beloved Son
for our salvation and our life.

We beseech you, Lord,
grant us throughout our earthly journey,
a spirit that does not bear grudges,
a pure conscience and sincere thoughts;
grant us also a heart capable of loving all our brothers.
Amen.

Peace: The Pattern of Unity

World Council of Churches (1959)

Meditation

By Him: peace passing understanding
With Him: peace among the peoples
In Him: peace in the Church
is to Thee
God the Father Almighty
in the
Unity of the Holy Ghost
All Honour and Glory

Daily Intention:

Resolving to be at peace this day: struggling for righteousness but trusting in God's judgment.

Remembering those under authority – magistrates and politicians, rulers and officials, those in military and diplomatic service, and all others who bear the burden of achieving and maintaining peace among men.

Visualizing what peace means for the unity of the Church.

The Unity of Love

Graymoor (1959)

O God, the Father,
Goodness surpassing all goodness,
Beauty surpassing beauty,

in Thee is tranquility, peace and concord.
Reconcile Thy servants who are separated from one another by dissensions,
and lead them back to the unity of the love
which conforms us to the image of Thy sublime nature.
And, even as Thou art above all things,
make us likewise one by generous unanimity of spirit.
So that, by the embrace of charity and the bonds of affection,
we may become spiritually one in our own souls
as well as with others,
in that peace which flows from Thee
and which makes all things serene,
in the grace, in the mercy, and in the love of Thy well-beloved Son.
Amen!

The 1960s

The 1960s were a decade of maturation for the ecumenical movement both for its various institutions and for the growing convergence in the movement of prayer for Christian unity. The Second Vatican Council (1962–1965) marked the Roman Catholic Church's official entry into the ecumenical movement, bringing an unprecedented gift to the movement for Christian unity. Canada hosted the Fourth World Conference on Faith and Order in 1963, and opened its doors to the world with Expo 67, a World's Fair held in Montreal in 1967 that coincided with the 100th anniversary celebrations of Canadian confederation. Culturally, the optimism, expansiveness and justice-seeking of the 1960s were counterbalanced by conflicts of many kinds, and the celebratory atmosphere was tinged with foreboding of war, nuclear threat and increasing global awareness of distress and poverty.

The full implications of the Second Vatican Council for ecumenism were not felt deeply until the later years of the decade. Yet already in 1961, in Canada for the first time, a Catholic representative attended Faith and Order Commission meetings as a most welcome observer. The introduction to the 1960 Week of Prayer materials from Faith and Order point to the scandal of differing views of the nature of prayer for Christian unity that still existed. The more Christians came to know each other, the more aware they were of the deep differences between them. The more prayer in common was needed, the more agencies of ecumenism needed to see that true unity in the Body of Christ is God's own work. The 1961 Faith and Order resources carried a strong sense of this paradoxical challenge, coupled with a strong missionary thrust.

Celebrating the upcoming New Delhi Assembly of the World Council of Churches in 1961, the call for prayer that year was also a call to repentance for the churches' self-satisfaction regarding their own efforts, for the Church's insensitivity to the real world, and for the half-heartedness of missionary efforts. Through the next few years, Faith and Order continued to call the churches to renewed service and mission. "What a narrow and ingrown society we have let the Church become!" chided the Week of Prayer resources in 1963, a firm reminder of the temptation to become institutionally self-focused even in the doing of God's work. Prayer is about God's will being done – opening ourselves so that God will work in, through and among us. Christians were asked to pray that God will give us the unity Christ asked God for: unity in truth and love, unity for witness and service.

Within the structures of the Canadian Council of Churches, the Week of Prayer for Christian Unity resources were produced by the Department of Evangelism. This "Week of Prayer and Witness" was to take place during the first week of January. While the Montreal Ecumenical Centre continued to distribute the materials from the Centre Unité in Lyon, the CCC created booklets that enlarged upon the Faith and Order resources for each year, including additional bible studies and prayers. In 1966, the CCC materials brought together the idea of the Week of Prayer for Christian Unity (January 18–25) and the Week of Prayer and Witness. The Week of Prayer called for a renewed *listening to* one another. An in-depth study of the Apostles' Creed was the focus of that year's Week of Prayer. In 1968, the CCC began collaborating with Novalis to produce an annual Canadian service adapted from the Faith and Order text.

There was a spirit of joy and celebration within the churches and in the ecumenical movement in the 1960s. It is a sign of maturity that the Week of Prayer for Christian Unity maintained a prophetic, challenging realism at the centre of Christian consciousness. The Centre Unité in Lyon continued to provide that prophetic voice:

> So long as our separations do not weigh heavily on our hearts, so long as they do not awaken in us a suffering which partakes of that of Christ in the presence of sin, we make of Christian Unity but a problem, although perhaps a more interesting problem than others … It has been said that we can only really pray and work for the unity of Christians when our separations cause us to suffer intensely.

J.E. Scully

The Unity of the Local Congregation in the Unity of the Universal Church

World Council of Churches (1960)

And God has appointed in the church ... teachers

Read 2 Timothy 3:14–17 (also Deuteronomy 6:6-9).

As you pray think of learning and teaching as the transmitting and receiving of mysteries entrusted to us by God

- of abiding in what you have learned
- of honouring and loving your teachers who fostered faith by helping you to fathom the realms of truth
- of the home and family as the first place of teaching and learning
- of youth as the time of learning and the power of God to renew our youth so that we can continue to learn
- of teaching as life-giving through the creativeness of the Word
- of biblical truth as the ground and aim of all Christian education.

As you pray remember you are a member of the whole Body of Christ and in particular reflect on the Bible as the common textbook of all Christians.

Let us pray: Almighty God, who has entrusted Thy saving truth unto men, that they may teach it to others; we pray thee ever to send true shepherds and teachers to prepare and instruct Thy Church and make it into Thy people. Bless, we beseech Thee, the work of all who teach Thy truth throughout Thy holy Church, that we may all be brought to the faith and saved through Thy Gospel. *Amen.*

A New Creation of the Spirit

World Council of Churches (1961)

We are not called into reunion which implies a return to the past, but into Unity, a new creation of the Spirit which yet lies ahead. This Unity which is not yet, judges us now. We have to return the church which we have fashioned in our own image, into the hands of the Lord of the Church that He may re-fashion it in His likeness. Here is the Cross of the ecumenical movement, that the beloved form of the church through which we have received all that we know of Him must be nailed to the Cross with its Master, that it may rise again with Him, and rising may conquer the world.

Ecumenical Hospitality

World Council of Churches (1962)

Ecumenical charity covers a multitude of sins of division. Our Lord bids us to make each other feel at home, in the practical sense by being hospitable, in the spiritual sense by including each other in our intercession. As good servants of a manifold divine grace, we can heal our divisions by practising ecumenical hospitality, by welcoming members of other Churches so that we may serve them. We can do the same thing in ecumenical intercession, by taking the prayers and intentions of other Churches into our own worship and our own prayer. 'Remember to show hospitality. There are some who, by so doing, have entertained angels without knowing it.' (Hebr. 13: 2; *NEB*)

Prayers for Denominations

World Council of Churches (1962)

For Roman Catholics

O Lord Jesus Christ, who didst say to thine apostles: Peace I leave with you, my peace I give unto you; regard not our sins, but the faith of thy Church, and grant it that peace and unity which is agreeable to thy will; who livest and reignest with the Father and the Holy Spirit, one God, world without end. (*Roman Missal*)

For the Orthodox and other Eastern Churches

O Lord, we beseech thee to be mindful of thy Holy Catholic and Apostolic Church which reaches from one end of the world to the other. Grant peace to this Church which thou hast built up by the precious blood of thy Christ. Establish this holy dwelling even unto the consummation of the world. (*Liturgy of St. Basil*)

For Anglicans and Old Catholics

O God, the Father of our Lord Jesus Christ, our only Saviour, the Prince of Peace; give us grace seriously to lay to heart the great dangers we are in by our unhappy divisions. Take away all hatred and prejudice, and whatsoever else may hinder us from godly union and concord; that, as there is but one Body, and one Spirit, and one hope of our calling, one Lord, one Faith, one Baptism, one God and Father of us all, so we may henceforth be all of one heart, and of one soul, united in one holy bond of truth and peace, of faith and charity, and may with one mind and one mouth glorify thee, through Jesus Christ our Lord. (*Book of Common Prayer*)

For Lutherans, Presbyterians and Reformed

O Lord, who willest that all thy children should be one in thee, we pray thee for the unity of thy Church. Pardon all our pride and our lack of faith, of understanding and of charity, which are the cause of our divisions. Deliver us from our narrow-mindedness, from our bitterness, from our prejudices. Preserve us from considering as normal that which is a scandal to the world and an offence to thy love. Teach us to recognise the gifts of thy grace amongst all those who call upon thee. (*Liturgy of the Reformed Church of France*)

For Baptists, Congregationalists and Methodists

O God the Saviour, God of the universe, Sovereign and Creator of all that is, Father of the one and only Son, in him thou hast begotten thy living and true image, thou hast sent him to save the human race; through him thou hast called and won mankind. We beseech thee for thy people gathered here; send thy Holy Spirit and may the Lord Jesus come amongst them and speak to the minds of all and incline their hearts to faith; may he lead all souls to thee, thou God of mercy. Do thou take possession of thy people in this place, and gather them together into one flock through thine only Son Jesus Christ in the Holy Spirit, through whom be ascribed to thee glory and power, now and unto ages of ages. (*Euchology of Serapion*)

For all Christians for whom we have not already prayed in particular, and for members of united Churches

Remember, Lord thy Church, to deliver it from all evil and to perfect it in thy love. And gather it together from the four winds, even thy Church which has been sanctified, into thy kingdom which thou hast prepared for it; through Jesus Christ thy Son, our Lord and God, who lives and reigns with thee in the unity of the Holy Spirit unto ages of ages. (*Didache*)

For the unity of all mankind in the love and truth of Christ

Almighty God, who has given us grace at this time with one accord to make our common supplications unto thee, and dost promise that when two or three are gathered together in thy Name thou wilt grant their requests; fulfil now, O Lord, the desires and petitions of thy servants, as may be most expedient for them; granting us in this world knowledge of thy truth, and in the world to come life everlasting. (*Prayer of St. Chrysostom*)

True Peace

World Council of Churches (1963)

Theme: Let us be reconciled to God (II Corinthians 5:20)

Prayer: Lord God, beloved and heavenly Father, we are gathered in your presence to ask you to reveal yourself to us as the strong, true and almighty God, who fills our darkness with his light. May we see your powerful deeds among us. May all the nations of the earth witness your grace and your victory over sin and iniquity. May your peace come to live in the hearts of all humans and your justice live in the minds of all the world's peoples. Grant also that we may think only of you. Almighty King of the Universe, to the glory of your name. Amen.

Reading: John 20:19-23

Meditation: Christ appears among the disciples, saying the words, "Peace be with you." The disciples rejoice when they recognize him. True peace is with them in the presence of the one who has conquered death. They must now bring this peace to others and Christ arms them for their task. Just as God at one time created the first human by breathing on him, so Jesus makes new men of his disciples. It is not of their own initiative that they set out, but at the command given them by Jesus. Through the transformation he has effected in them, they place themselves at his service. He has even given them the authority to forgive sins. It is as if Jesus himself were walking the earth in the person of his disciples. He is peace and they bear witness to him by submitting to his will.

For the Roman Catholic Church

World Council of Churches (1964)

For the Roman Catholic Church – for its faithful members and its shepherds, particularly for those in positions of great responsibility – that the Holy Spirit may grant fruitful increase to the work and decisions of the Second Vatican Council.

Glory Be to Thee

Canadian Council of Churches (1964)

Leader. Let us give thanks to God:
> We thank thee, Father, for the life and knowledge which thou hast granted us through Jesus, thy Servant.

All: *Glory be to thee for ever and ever.*

L: We thank thee, Father, for thy holy name which thou hast hidden in our hearts, for the knowledge, faith and immortality which thou hast granted us through Jesus, thy Servant.

All: *Glory be to thee for ever and ever.*

L: We thank thee, Father, for the benefits which thou dost grant us in the ecumenical movement; for opening hearts and minds to the understanding and sharing of thy gifts in us and in our brethren through the Holy Spirit.

All: *Glory be to thee for ever and ever.*

L: We thank thee, Father, for the call to prayer for the unity of thy Church, for all those who are called by the inspiration of your Holy Spirit to devote themselves to the cause of unity.

All: *Glory be to thee for ever and ever.*

L: In the presence of our Lord Jesus Christ, let us repent and confess our sins against unity: For the little importance that we have given to this word proceeding from thy heart "Other sheep I have which are not of this fold; them also I must bring; they shall hear my voice …"

All: *We beseech thee to pardon us, O Lord.*

L: For our controversies, sometimes full of irony, narrow-mindedness or exaggeration with regard to our Christian brethren, for our intransigence and our harsh judgments,

All: *We beseech thee to pardon us, O Lord.*

L: For all the restrictive measures unjustly taken against them,

All: *We beseech thee to pardon us, O Lord.*

L: For all self-sufficiency and pride which we have shown to our Christian brethren over the centuries and for all our lack of understanding towards them,

All: *We beseech thee to pardon us, O Lord.*

L: For bad example of our conduct, which has hindered, diminished or destroyed the effect of grace in the souls of all our Christian brethren,

All: *We beseech thee to pardon us, O Lord.*

L: For our neglect of frequent, fervent and brotherly prayer for them,

All: *We beseech thee to pardon us, O Lord.*

L: May the Holy Spirit guide our prayer for unity towards Jesus and the Father: Beyond the frontiers of language, race and nation,

All: *Unite us, Lord Jesus.*

L: Beyond our ignorances, our prejudices and our instinctive enmities,

All: *Unite us, Lord Jesus.*

L: Beyond our intellectual and spiritual barriers,

All: *Unite us, Lord Jesus.*

L: O God, for thy greater glory,

All: *Gather together all separated Christians.*

L: O God, that goodness and truth may prevail,

All: *Gather together all separated Christians.*

L: O God, that there may be only one flock and one Shepherd,

All: *Gather together all separated Christians.*

L: O God, that Satan's pride may be confounded,

All: *Gather together all separated Christians.*

L: O God, so that peace may at last reign on earth,

All: *Gather together all separated Christians.*

L: O God, for the greater joy of thy Son,

All: *Gather together all separated Christians.*

For Peace, Brotherhood, and Loving-Kindness in the World

Canadian Council of Churches (1964)

O God, Who didst make of one blood all nations of men,

    Make mankind to love one another;

In the name of Prince of Peace,

    Break in pieces the weapons of war;

In the name of humanity's King,

Deliver the peoples from the rule of greed;

    By the Gospel of the Kingdom of love and truth,

Rid of us hatred and lies;

    As Thou hast made all races and peoples of one family,

Keep us from shedding our brother's blood;

    As our Lord loved little children and took them in His arms,

Save them from mangled bodies and twisted minds.

O God, save the people!

Love

When his eyes were opened by love John looked back at the Last Supper and introduced it with the words, "Having loved His own which were in the world, He loved them to the end." It was not to the end of life, but to the end of love itself, to the limits of limitless love. He loved us before we were born so that we are "planned" people. He loves us all through life, and in the last hour His love welcomes us to the eternal fold.

Faith

The Trinity is not an arrangement of bloodless categories; it is the family of God; it is the social concept of God. More, it is a way of living. It is a great mystery which breaks through language and escape. Yet without the Trinity God will be too small.

Thought

Praise pulls the soul out from selfishness, out from the dark corners of introspection, into a life of appreciation. Even as Shakespeare thought ingratitude the meanest of the vices, so gratitude and appreciation are marks of a magnanimous, great-hearted personality.

All Things New
World Council of Churches (1965)

Behold, I make all things new (Revelation 21:5)

Tens of thousands of people all over the world now pray for Christian unity during this week especially, and this leaflet is an invitation to join in that prayer which in the first place is Christ's own prayer to the Father. Yet this prayer for unity is a waste of time unless we are convinced:

that God has made all things new: through the coming of Jesus Christ among us and the gift of his Spirit he has opened up new possibilities for mankind and for the whole creation;

and that God can renew our churches and ourselves day by day: all prayer is in one sense an act of trust in his power to renew us. But our generation in particular has been guided to see that Christian renewal is not just an individual matter: it involves the wholeness of Christ's Church and the wholeness of human society. Let us therefore pray for:

the unity which Christ asked from God,
unity in truth and love,
unity for witness and service.

Seventh Day – Theme: "I will write on him … my own new name." (Revelation 3:12)

Prayer

Our Father, who hast made all men in thy likeness and lovest all whom thou has made, suffer not our family to separate itself from thee by building barriers of race and colour. As thy Son our Saviour was born of a Hebrew mother, but rejoiced in the faith of a Syrian woman and of a Roman soldier, welcomed the Greeks who sought him, and suffered a man from Africa to carry his cross, so teach us to regard the members of all races as fellow-heirs in the kingdom of Jesus Christ our Lord. *Amen.*

Lessons: Isaiah 12; Revelation 3:7-13

Meditation: "I will write on him ... my own new name." So Christ promises a new name to those who conquer. And when Christ gives a new name to his Church in any locality, that means he takes complete possession of it as its Lord. But Christianity is divided into numerous churches, each bearing its own name. Is this the name given it by Christ, or one which we have given to ourselves? Does not the very multiplicity of names show to what a great degree Christianity lives in self-will and disobedience? Just as Christ called upon the church in Philadelphia to keep his word, in order that it might receive his new name, so he calls us not to be attached at all costs to the name which we give ourselves, but to grow in holiness so that we may receive *his* new name.

Intercession

For the proclamation of the good news of Jesus Christ in all lands – for a renewal of missionary responsibility in the churches – for all those who take seriously the command to go and preach the gospel and who give their strength to this task – for unity in the Christian mission:

Lord, have mercy. Christ, have mercy. Lord, have mercy.

Eighth Day – Theme: Sing to the Lord a new song; sing to the Lord, all the earth! (Psalm 96:1)

Act of Dedication

We confess Jesus Christ, Saviour of men and the light of the world.
Together we accept his command;
We commit ourselves anew to bear witness to him among men;
We offer ourselves to serve all men in love, that love which he alone imparts;
We accept afresh our calling to make visible our unity in him;
We pray for the gift of the Holy Spirit for our task.

Lessons: Psalm 96; Revelation 5:6–14

Meditation

We are here called upon to "sing a new song" – new because God himself is always newly at work amongst us. When we speak of Christ we are not speaking of an old story which took place in the dim past. Rather is he the Lord who holds all things in his hands, who offers us his salvation today, and who will come to judge the world. Thus the Church of Christ is that community which is always able to sing a new song to God. Here is the psalmist's challenge to us now; are we able to join in that song and to sing in such a way that our music does not embrace the Church only, but resounds through the whole world?

Intercession

For the peace of the whole world – for governments and international organizations – that the peace of Christ may prevail in all racial and national conflicts – for justice for the oppressed, the hungry and those dispossessed of their rights – for the witness of the Church in the life of all peoples:

Lord, have mercy. Christ, have mercy. Lord, have mercy.

On the Apostles' Creed

Canadian Council of Churches (1966)

Dorothy L. Sayers, that brilliant writer of detective stories, some little time ago wrote a booklet called "Creed or Chaos." In this booklet she makes a most interesting observation: that the Roman Catholic Church is a theological society in a sense in which the Anglican Church (her own Church) is not, and that, because of this insistence on theology, the Roman Catholic Church is a disciplined body, honoured and sociologically important …

Let us get this straight, that the Apostles' Creed was never intended to be literally and microscopically examined as hard, cold statements of logical reasoning and scientific fact. (Didn't St. Paul say something about the foolishness of preaching the cross?) The Apostles' Creed is really poetry. It is a desperate attempt to declare to the world what cannot after all be put into statements and propositions …

Believing in God the Father means simply that our selfishness and sins do not so much break the laws of God; they break the heart of God. (In simple fact, there is no such thing as breaking the laws of God: They remain as steadfast and strong as ever; rather it is we, the transgressors, who are broken!) "Sin," someone has cried, "sin is the raised voice and the clenched fist and the blow in the face of God" …

Just this also: God is our Heavenly Father, not our doting grandfather. Firmness and sternness and high and hard demands are a part of all true love …

[B]elieving in the divinity of Jesus is more than just a matter of doctrine; it is a matter of morality. Is my life lived from day to day as if Jesus were "my Lord and my God"?

Glory and Light

Canadian Council of Churches (1966)

I will be their God, and they shall be my people (Ezekiel 37:27)

Only twenty years ago a quite small number of people – of different Christian denominations – were convinced that they ought to pray *specially* (though such prayers already existed, of course, in the liturgies regularly used by many Churches) for Christian unity. To-day we have evidence that probably millions in every continent of the world are joining in this prayer; and this leaflet is an invitation to you to do the same. Numbers do not matter very much; what matters is that Christians should pray in harmony for their Lord's known will for his Church – that they should care more and more, as he did,

for the union of all his people,
in love towards one another and in witness to the world.

Eighth Day – Theme: They shall be his people, and God himself … will be their God (Revelation 21:3)

Lessons: Hosea 2:16-23; Revelation 21:1-7

Meditation: The Church is represented in glory, as a bride adorned for her marriage. God has changed her heart. He can now be united with her in a mutual exchange of love, adopt her children definitely as his own, dwell with her forever, and refresh her from the very source of life. The glorification of the people of God sheds its light over the whole creation which itself is transfigured. This light, which shines upon humanity in its state of perfection and of entire harmony with God, should certainly never deflect us from our present painful efforts to forge a new and better likeness for the Church. But our labour is performed with a light heart, since we already taste the first fruits of that world to come. We are united in the remembrance of our Lord, in proclaiming the mystery of the marriage of the Lamb, and in awaiting his return. Must we not then grow more and more in the love of Christ "until his coming again"?

Intercession: For the peace of the whole world – for governments and international organizations – that the peace of Christ may prevail in all racial and national conflicts – for justice for the oppressed, the hungry, and those dispossessed of their rights – for the witness of the Church in the life of all peoples:

Lord, have mercy. Christ, have mercy. Lord, have mercy.

Prayer

O Lord our God, who hast bidden the light to shine out of darkness, who hast again wakened us to praise thy goodness and ask for thy grace; accept now, in thy endless mercy, the sacrifice of our worship and thanksgiving, and grant unto us all such requests as may be wholesome for us. Make us to be children of the light and of the day, and heirs of thy everlasting inheritance. Remember, O Lord, according to the multitude of thy mercies, thy whole Church; all who join with us in prayer, all our brethren, on land or sea, or wherever they may be in thy vast kingdom, who stand in need of thy grace and succour. Pour out upon them the riches of thy mercy, so that we with them, redeemed in soul and body, and steadfast in faith, may ever praise thy wonderful and holy name; through Jesus Christ our Lord. *Amen. (Liturgy of St. James)*

The Divided Members of Thy Flock Unite

Graymoor (1967)

Lord our God; we praise thee that thou art the holy God who doest great wonders. We thank thee for the wonder of our meeting in a world divided. We thank thee for the wonder of reconciliation in a world of revenge. We thank thee for the wonder of love in a world of hatred. We thank thee for the wonder of light when we go astray. Let the life which thy Son has revealed and given to us, grow stronger in every member of thy body until thou art known as the life of all men and the hope of the whole world; to the glory of thy name. Amen. (*Evangelical Youth, Germany*)

O God, whose nature and whose ways are goodness, giver of quietness and peace, grant to thy Church the gift of peace and rest which cannot be broken. Reconcile those who are at variance and unite the divided members of thy flock, so that we may keep fast thy peace as an anchor of faith in our souls. Give us concord with one another, and join us together into a holy temple, built up in perfect unity, through Jesus Christ our Lord. Amen. (*Maruthas of Tancrit, Liturgy*)

Spirit of the Living Christ, come upon us in the glory of thy risen power; Spirit of the Living Christ, come upon us in all the humility of thy wondrous love; Spirit of the Living Christ, come upon us that new life may course within our veins, new love bind us together in one family, a new vision of the Kingdom of God spur us on to serve thee with fearless passion. For thy sake we ask it. Amen. (*Iona Community*)

Living Hope

Centre for Ecumenism, Montreal (1967)

Since Christ's resurrection there is a living hope (1 Peter 1:3-9), and the possession of this hope can be compared to a new birth. Nobody can cause his own natural birth. In the same way, the new birth is God's gift. For through His resurrection Christ broke through the boundaries which lead into the future, and He gives us a share in this victory. The more we share in His breakthrough into the future, the more shall we be united with one another; for thus we grow in our faith and therefore grow together.

The full meaning of this living hope will be visible only in the last day. The present time is mostly marked by affliction and suffering. Every Christian, every church has to bear the contradiction between this hope and present experiences. But the living hope is stronger than the passing danger. It unites those who suffer, and ensures that the tribulations are recognized as tests of their faith. Christians therefore receive comfort and give it likewise to the others. In the mutual comfort to be found among Christians, God has given us a strong bond of unity (II Cor. 1:3-7). Again, throughout the ages, He fulfills those promises for which Christians are waiting the fulfillment. But they do not wait only for their own sakes. God's plan for His people includes the salvation of the whole world also.

The Christian Pavilion at Expo '67 will depict dimensions which are part of man's life – it will show some of the great achievements of our era and come to grips with seemingly insurmountable problems, suffering and sadness – and it will show how Christianity is an integral part of our modern society, and Christ's message one of Truth and Hope for all men.

Called to One Hope

The actuality of the Christian Pavilion midst "Man and His World" is a prophetic gesture. The Pavilion will prove that Christians of different confessions, notwithstanding their divisions, are able to unite in an act of faith and love so as to present to mankind common testimony of hope. All true Christians regret the present divisions and hope for ever more perfect reconciliation. Is not this search for unity, that which is desired by God? Is it not the chief source of hope for contemporary man?

Prayer for the Christian Pavilion, Expo '67

Centre for Ecumenism, Montreal (1967)

Lord Jesus Christ, You, who inspired the Churches of Canada to a concerted effort in the presentation of your Good News to "Man and His World," give your grace to those who are preparing the Christian Pavilion for Expo '67.

To repair our past intolerance, we offer you the concrete sacrifices we must undergo today in order to come to a better mutual understanding and love.

Since You want us to be one that the world may believe, show us how to unite in making the Christian Pavilion a manifestation of Your Salvation to the men of our day.

Help us to overcome the barriers, whether cultural, psychological or administrative, which arise between us … barriers which often tend to separate us more surely than do our theological differences.

Give us the grace to avoid the tone which strives to impose a personal opinion, the phrase which recalls a forgotten division, the word which hurts, the vain or empty argument, the intrigue which divides into opposing camps, all fear of assuming responsibility, and futile delay in taking necessary decisions.

Take from our minds and hearts all that can delay the building of the Christian Pavilion and the attainment of unity. Amen.

The Christian Pavilion Prayer

Canadian Council of Churches (1967)

Lord Jesus Christ,
Light shining in the darkness,
You have shared the life of man in his world.

Faithful to Your prayer for unity,
We, Your disciples and Your brothers,
By the grace of Your spirit,
Wish to give to the world Your message of hope.

By Your coming and Your presence
Your have created a new world
Into which You have called us to live.

May our Pavilion proclaim this good news
And guide men in their search for God.

By Your birth and Your living among us,
By Your death and Your resurrection,
You have given direction to our life.

Send Your Spirit upon the visitors to our Pavilion,
That they may be led to discover,
Through the grandeur and the misery of this world,
the mystery of Your coming among men and of their salvation.

You have told Your disciples
To love the Father, to love one another,
To love all men and to serve them all.

May this Pavilion recall Your message of love.
May it make you known, You who have said:
I am the Way, the Truth and the Life.

May Your love for men
Illuminate our faith and be our hope;
Grant that we share our faith and hope
With those who are looking for You.

For All Christians

Second Vatican Council, celebration of 4 December 1965,
at St. Paul-without-the-walls
World Council of Churches (1968)

Lord Jesus Christ, in you we see the Father's love – the love he gives us in the Spirit – and in that love we pray

- for all Christians, that they may renew their hope in the power of your Father who loves the world and saves it

- for all men; that in the hour and by the means you choose, you will unite them to yourself in love and truth.

Response: *O Lord, hear our prayer*

May our prayer rise to your glorious throne, O Lord, and may our request not return to us unheeded. Unite our lips and our hearts in praise and repentance so that one day, in the fullness of the communion of your Church, we may advance together towards your kingdom, which has no end. Through Christ our Lord. Amen.

Called to Freedom

(World Council of Churches, 1969)

First Day

Theme: Christ has set us free (Galatians 5:1)

Bible readings: Exodus 2:23–3:12, Galatians 4:1-7, 5:1

God is a God who sets his people free. The promise of deliverance from slavery in Egypt came through Moses to Israel of old. Now in Christ, through the Spirit, the promise of freedom and sonship is being fulfilled for us and for all mankind.

Second Day

Theme: Where the Spirit of the Lord is, there is freedom (II Corinthians 3:17)

Bible readings: Isaiah 61:1-4, 11; II Corinthians 3:1-6

The freedom of the people of God is brought to fruition by his Spirit, at work in creation and re-creation. It is he who brings us into the freedom of the new covenant in Christ.

Third Day

Theme: The truth will make you free (John 8:32)

Bible readings: Ezekiel 36:24-28; John 8:31-36

Freedom is not something we control or which circumstances can guarantee. It is God's gift, as we live by his forgiveness in Christ and obey his truth. Otherwise we remain slaves.

Fourth Day

Theme: Reconciling the world (II Corinthians 5:19)

Bible readings: Isaiah 49:5-13; II Corinthians 5:17–6:2

The freedom by which Christians live is not just from themselves but for the world: it thrusts them out to share God's mission of redemption to all mankind, for which Christ came.

Fifth Day

Theme: Through love be servants of one another (Galatians 5:13)

Bible readings: Jeremiah 34:8-17; Galatians 5:13-26

Christian freedom is something we can fully possess only as we give it back, as the servant-community of Christ, in loving service of our brothers – seeking their freedom rather than our own.

Sixth Day

Theme: You have not withheld your son (Genesis 22:16)

Bible readings: Genesis 22:1-18; Mark 8:31-35

Christian freedom involves freedom for suffering and sacrifice: Abraham's offering of his son points forward to God's self-giving in Christ, who freely chose to endure the Cross. That is our calling too.

Seventh Day

Theme: Freedom builds up (I Corinthians 10:23)

Bible readings: Isaiah 58:6-12; I Corinthians 10:23-33

Christian freedom spends itself in strong compassion for the weak and oppressed. Its concern is not with scruples about behaviour or ritual, but with upbuilding – with the Kingdom which is "righteousness and peace and joy in the Holy Spirit."

Eighth Day

Theme: The final freedom (Romans 8:21)

Bible readings: Isaiah 40:1-11; Romans 8:14-25

The day will come when the glorious liberty of the children of God shines through the whole creation, restored at last to unity and freedom. For that day we wait and work in the patience of hope.

The 1970s

The Week of Prayer for Christian Unity movement had much to say to the "Me Generation." In the context of a culture of increasing validation of individualism and competition, prayers lifted up gratitude for God's gift of community in Christ and in the household of God. They encouraged Christians to engage in the world, organize themselves in service, and build community within and across the churches. In the shock of the fragility of this time, with growing secularism, increasing and rapid technological advance and the continued stress of nuclear threat, the churches and the ecumenical movement faced the challenge of "relevance."

The Week of Prayer resources open the decade by reminding the churches that unity is the work of the Holy Spirit drawing us into communion with one another, not something we accomplish on our own. Let us not be afraid of the differences we find, but answer the call of the Spirit to become even closer to each other, and that Spirit will draw us together and out in service to the world. The Canadian Week of Prayer resources, now a joint project involving the Canadian Council of Churches and the Canadian Catholic Conference, developed creative resources to equip local communities in engaging in ecumenical celebration and learning. Mutual learning, development of friendships and cooperation in social service were all encouraged through concrete suggestions and, at the heart of it all, prayer. "Prayer for this unity is the soul of the ecumenical movement, and the measure of concern for unity," offered the joint letter of the Presidents of the Canadian Council of Churches and the Canadian Catholic Conference.

An ecumenical conference on evangelism in 1970 opened doors for new developments in common mission in Canada. That year, following the first walk on the moon in 1969, the service booklets featured a photograph of the moon – a new view that changed our perceptions forever.

By 1971, a joint working group linking the Canadian Catholic Conference and the Canadian Council of Churches was consulting regularly. The Coalition for Development was growing. The Presbyterian, Lutheran, United, Roman Catholic and Anglican churches were finding an increasing number of common projects in social justice and witness, out of which would eventually grow the social justice ecumenical coalitions. Community building at local and national institutional levels for mission, service and advocacy was the hallmark of much of church life. What a contrast to the "Me Generation" values! Contrary to the sort of pluralism being celebrated in the culture, ecumenism calls us to something deeper. The 1971 Week of Prayer for Christian Unity explains, "True ecumenism is not equivalent to a perpetual pluralism in which each seeks his own. It is, rather, a movement that, while accepting legitimate diversity, is marked by a dynamic convergence in, obedient and joyful response to, the authentic inspiration of the Holy Spirit."

The prayers and bible studies offered in the Week of Prayer for Christian Unity did not shy away from addressing growing secularism, individualism and the question of "relevance" of the Christian message. A meditation on 1 Peter 4:7-11 in 1979 addressed these issues directly. Reflecting on the isolation of Christians across Turkey as described in 1 Peter, the authors point to the sustaining and unifying power of Christian faith.

> In a society where Christian values count for little, are you aware of similar support by and for your fellow Christians – at work? – in your street? Or don't you even know who they are? In a world of tensions and fears, the people of God are called on to build up bonds of peace and love. Many people are full of fear of impending doom, but our lives and service and the transformation of our church structures should bear witness to what it means to live in the creative tension of trust and hope. As Christians we claim that, in Christ, the Kingdom of God, the new creation, has *already* come, but we also claim that there will come a time when this will break through, and in it the whole of creation will find, not its destruction, but its fulfillment.

> *J.E. Scully*

That There May Be Peace

Canadian Council of Churches / Canadian Catholic Conference (1970)

Leader: Let us pray for one another:
> That there may be peace in our hearts, harmony in our homes, justice and love in our institutions, mutual respect and co-operation in society. Let us pray to the Lord.

Response: *Lord, hear our prayer.*

L: Let us pray for openness:
> That, in an atmosphere of openness, effective communication may be established between employees and employers, between the poor and the rich, between those under authority and those holding authority, between persons of different age groups, different cultures, different creeds and different attitudes. Let us pray to the Lord.

R: *Lord, hear our prayer.*

L: Let us pray for renewal and effective action:
> That the common good be always served by political, economic, social and religious attitudes which acknowledge the dignity of the person and take into account the particular needs of our society. Let us pray to the Lord.

R: *Lord, hear our prayer.*

L: Let us pray for Christian unity:
> That, under the guidance of the Holy Spirit, every Christian, every home, every parish, every community, every organization, every Church, may work for the recovery of the unity and brotherly love, that God wills. Let us pray to the Lord.

R: *Lord, hear our prayer.*

God Is Speaking to Us

Graymoor (1970)

Man finds considerable difficulty today in recognizing the presence of God in a world which is increasingly shaped by his own activity, but is he not, through this very situation, being called to new responsibilities in a demanding and stimulating way? We may discover that not only are we searching for God but that God is speaking to us in the reality of the world. God speaks to us when our neighbor calls for bread, for work, for health or for education. He asks us as he asked Cain, "Where is your brother?" (cf. Gen. 4:9).

Welcoming People of Every Race

Centre Unité Chrétienne, Lyon (1971)

Lord Jesus Christ, you were born of a Jewish mother, but you rejoiced greatly in the faith shown by a Syrian woman and a Roman soldier; you welcomed with kindness the Greeks who sought you, and you let an African man carry your cross. Grant us also that we may welcome people of every race into your kingdom as co-heirs. (*Lutheran Church, Zulu*)

Co-ordinating Our Energies

Canadian Council of Churches / The Canadian Catholic Conference (1971)

The universal Week of Prayer for Christian Unity constitutes a most appropriate time for us to speak again of the urgency of the call of Christ that we should be united in a world which is entitled to receive from us a witness of brotherly solidarity in the same faith of the Gospel.

The Spirit of Christ constantly entreats us to unite ourselves in prayer and to co-ordinate our energies in order to find solutions for the numerous human problems in which together we have the responsibility to be interested.

We invite you, fellow Christians, to co-operate with all those who are in charge of preparing for the Week of Unity and of assuring a lively celebration of it throughout Canada.

A.B.B. Moore, President, The Canadian Council of Churches
J.A. Plourde, President, The Canadian Catholic Conference

United by the Spirit

Canadian Council of Churches / Canadian Catholic Conference (1971)

When the Apostles boldly proclaimed the work of universal salvation accomplished by Jesus Christ;

When the first Christians accepted martyrdom in order to establish firmly the liberating expansion of the gospel message in the world;

When a Dag Hammarskjold, a John XXIII, a Martin Luther King and many others work, even to giving up their lives, to bring men together;

When students, workers and professional people truly exert themselves in the cause of justice, peace and unity in their neighbourhood and in the world;

When in a society that is rapidly changing, a converging desire is being felt to see charity triumphing over hate, union over conflicts, hope over despair … *it is the HOLY SPIRIT who is at work.*

It is the unifying Spirit delivered up by Christ at the moment of his death upon the cross: "He delivered up the Spirit." (John 19:30) Indeed, Jesus "received the Holy Spirit, the object of the promise, and has poured it forth." (Acts 2:33)

The role of the Holy Spirit is to sanctify and to bring together those who believe in Christ, and through them, to bring about a much greater coming together of all men.

It is for this reason that our divisions between Christians constitute a contrary witness:

> The objections of those who believe that they do not find any response in the Church to their needs for true brotherhood must be taken seriously. The communion of the Holy Spirit is only genuine when the community practices fellowship in a fraternal spirit, when it is concerned to discover the truth, when it is the setting for freedom.

Christians of today, is it not our common responsibility to rediscover the unifying function of the Spirit in the Church and in the world?

Some Encouraging Examples of Ecumenism in Canada

- A Joint Working Group linking the Canadian Catholic Conference and the Canadian Council of Churches for regular consultation, common planning and action. In the context of the Canadian situation, the group is bilingual.

- The Christian Pavilion at "EXPO '67," the project of seven Canadian Churches and continued since 1968 as a public witness in "Man and His World."

- Joint planning and action in regard to poverty and development between the Roman Catholic and member Churches of the Canadian Council during Lent of 1970 and to be continued in 1971 and in the future; also, re the on-going work of the Coalition for Development.

- Many local examples across Canada of joint inner-city social work, joint use of sanctuaries for worship and other forms of service, common planning and action in meeting community needs.

- Wide participation in such projects as The Churchmen's Seminar, Ottawa; Theological Commissions; the 1970 Conference on Evangelism; co-operation in theological education.

- Increasing participation on the part of all Canadian Churches in various joint activities during the "Week of Prayer for Christian Unity."

Convergence

In loyalty to Jesus Christ and in response to His prayer "That all may be one," we must seek to do together all that we can do together and grow in an understanding of ever wider fields of cooperation and sharing than those we presently acknowledge. We must work together to give witness to Christ and His will for the world, thus anticipating the final reconciliation of all men with each other and with God. Our objective should be "Together – not just side by side."

True ecumenism is not equivalent to a perpetual pluralism in which each seeks his own. It is, rather, a movement that, while accepting legitimate diversity, is marked by a dynamic convergence in obedient and joyful response to the authentic inspirations of the Holy Spirit.

Sharing in the same faith and the same love, united in the same Spirit and the same hope, let us lift up to God our joint prayer.

Intentions

1. Holy Father, who creates the universe and makes man in your own image, grant that all Christians may realize their calling.

   Response: *Keep us, O Lord, in your love.*

2. Holy Father, who calls all men to the unity of a single family, forgive our acts of division.

   R: *Keep us, O Lord, in your love.*

3. Holy Father, who at the end of time will make all things new, grant that the churches may prepare the world for that glorious day.

   R: *Keep us, O Lord, in your love.*

4. O Lord Jesus, who was born into a human family, grant that through your presence among us we may live together in one brotherhood.

   R: *Keep us, O Lord, in your love.*

5. O Lord Jesus, who died in order to gather into one people the scattered children of God, teach us to be truly sorry for the scandal of our divisions

   R: *Keep us, O Lord, in your love.*

6. O Lord, who by your resurrection triumphed over death, lead all men out of the darkness into the light.

   R: *Keep us, O Lord, in your love.*

7. O Holy Spirit, who changed the hearts of the apostles, grant that all Christians may live for others.

   R. *Keep us, O Lord, in your love.*

8. O Holy Spirit, who leads the church into all truth, help us to search out the truths we have not yet learned to see.

   R. *Keep us, O Lord, in your love.*

9. O Holy Spirit, who awakens the heart of love, grant that we may obey those commandments which we have been content only to hear.

   R. *Keep us, O Lord, in your love.*

Unite Us, Lord Jesus

Graymoor (1973)

Leader: May the Holy Spirit make us to understand the prayer that Jesus offered for his people: "That they all may be one, as thou Father in me and I in thee; that the world may believe that thou hast sent me."

Leader: Beyond our ignorances, our prejudices, and our traditional enmities,

All: *Unite us, Lord Jesus.*

L: Beyond our intellectual and spiritual barriers,

All: *Unite us, Lord Jesus.*

L: Beyond the frontiers of language, race and nation,

All: *Unite us, Lord Jesus.*

Act of Penitence

Canadian Council of Churches / Canadian Conference of Catholic Bishops (1973)

We confess to Almighty God and to each other

That we have sinned through our own fault

   In our thoughts and in our words

   In what we have done and in what we have failed to do

In recognizing and maintaining the unity of your Church.

We ask you to fill us with your Holy Spirit.
　　Make us whole again
　　Renew your Church in the world
　　Restore us in honor
Through Jesus Christ who reveals God to man
and reconciles man to God.

Jesus is Lord!

Canadian Council of Churches / Canadian Catholic Conference (1974)

Leader: Go forth, O Christian people
　　　　in the name of God the Father who made you,
　　　　in the name of God the Son who redeemed you,
　　　　in the name of the Spirit who makes you holy.
　　　　Go forth and teach the world by your love
　　　　that you are united in following Christ.

The Tree of the Cross

(National Council of Churches / Graymoor, 1974)

Blessed be you, O Lord,
Father of our Lord Jesus Christ,
who has blessed us with all sorts of spiritual benedictions
through your Son.
Between heaven and earth reconciled
you have erected the tree of the cross:
Let its branches reach out
to the most distant points of the earth
so that its fruit might cure all the nations,
that its light might guide men along the road to salvation,
that the peoples gathered in Christ might praise you forevermore.

Confession

Canadian Council of Churches (1975)

Leader: By reconciling us to God,
    Jesus frees us, and makes us one.

All: *By reconciling us to God, Jesus frees us, and makes us one.*

L: Have mercy on us, O God, have mercy,
    for in you have we taken refuge.
    We call to God the most high,
    to God, who has always been our helper.
    May God in heaven come to save us,
    sending us his love and truth.

All: *By reconciling us to God, Jesus frees us, and makes us one.*

L: Our hearts are ready, O God,
    our hearts are ready.
    We will sing your praises.

All: *By reconciling us to God, Jesus frees us, and makes us one.*

Leader: We will thank you among the nations, Lord,
    praise you before all men,
    for your love reaches to the skies,
    your truth to the heavens above.

All: *By reconciling us to God, Jesus frees us, and makes us one.*

(From Psalm 57)

Renewal of the Baptismal Promises

Graymoor (1975)

Leader: We were buried with Christ in baptism,
    so that as Christ was raised from the dead by the Father's glory,
    we too might walk in newness of life.
    You are God's people,
    so that you may declare the wonderful deeds of him who called you out of darkness
    into his marvelous light.

There is one body and one Spirit,
just as you were called to the one hope that belongs to your call,
one Lord, one faith, one baptism, one God and Father of us all.
Therefore
will you again renew the promises made in your baptism?
will you accept again the new life which God gives in Christ?
and will you continue to serve God faithfully in his holy Church?

(here follows the proclaiming of the Nicene Creed)

All: *We accept anew Christ Jesus as our Savior and Lord;*
We acknowledge and affirm the faith by which the Church lives;
We celebrate our unity with all who share in the one baptism:
We love and trust God, the Father of our Lord Jesus Christ and our Father;
By his grace we are made his People; to him be glory forever. Amen.

The Olympics: A Call to Excel

Canadian Council of Churches / Canadian Catholic Conference (1976)

The coming event of the Olympic Games, in our own country, is an invitation to explore the ways of excellence, which they should normally symbolize.

The athlete, subject to a fairly rigid discipline and striving towards victory, is a specialist in physical prowess. In the same way, the Christian, as a follower of Christ, is a specialist in human excellence. Already, Saint Paul, addressing the Corinthians, suggested the parallel: *"Do you not know that in a race all the runners compete, but only one receives the prize? So run that you may obtain it. Every athlete exercises self-control in all things. They do it to receive a perishable wreath, but we an imperishable."* (1 Cor. 9:24-25). The real life of the baptized should be a manifestation of victory over sin and a proclamation of the life of glory to which he has been raised.

The Olympic Games provide a very favorable occasion and context to reflect on *"man in motion"* and on the role and place of sports in a civilization of leisure time activities. Beyond and through the '76 event, the attention of the Christian churches and the polarization of their ministry should be directed first towards human beings. The games pass, the athlete remains, and the Church's mission goes on.

The evangelization of the world of sport cannot come about except in an ecumenical perspective, in the respect for men from diverse cultures and religions. At a time when the Olympic spectacle is of paramount present interest, would it not be the opportune moment "to say and do together everything that can be said and done together" in regard to sports?

To place the dynamism of our faith at the service of authentic sports values: strength and beauty of body, attention, judgment, self-control, endurance, a zest for effort and success, respect for others, team spirit, loyalty, docility, justice, modesty, compliance with the rules of the game, etc., is already a way of witnessing to our Christian mystique: it is already an announcement of the Good News.

"Faster, higher, stronger" is the motto which animates the athlete's ideal, symbolized by the Olympic flame; could it not act as a catalyzer in the race which Saint Paul invites us to undertake with him on the road to excellence?

God's Gift and Wish for All
Canadian Council of Churches / Canadian Catholic Conference (1977)

Father, we celebrate the peace which
your Son has come to bring
in a world that is not yet at peace.
We celebrate the love you have shown
to a world that is still filled with hate.
In this unfinished world, which is our home,
you have given us work to do:
to be instruments of peace, symbols of unity, signs of hope.
May what we do today speak that word of peace, unity and hope,
which is your gift and wish for all. Amen.

Daily Prayer
Canadian Council of Churches / Canadian Conference of Catholic Bishops (1978)

Heavenly Father,

In your Son, Jesus Christ,
You revealed to us the way, the truth and the life.
Through Him, you commanded us to love one another.

In Him,
may we find, all of us
– citizens of different origins, in a rapidly changing Canada –
guidance, inspiration, confidence!

May your Spirit lead us
>> to practice mutual respect;
>> may He help us to understand and to support one another!

Strengthened by your help,
>> with daring and perseverance,
>> may we build together,
>> for the common good of our fellow-citizens,
>> a new society founded on truth, justice and love!

Act of Reconciliation

Graymoor (1979)

Speaker: We have – in the past and until today – not always served one another, but fought one another, ignored one another, and thus contributed to the scandal of the division of Christ's body. Pray, therefore, for God's forgiveness.

Leader/Liturgist: Lord, though we are still sinners, you have never ceased to love us or to take pity on us. With the words of Peter the apostle, we call to you.

Congregation: *Lord, you know everything; you know that we love you.*

L: Lord, like the apostle Peter, we have also trusted more in ourselves than in your grace. But you, Lord, turn to us and have pity.

C: *Lord, you know everything; you know that we love you.*

L: We have been proud, and we have considered ourselves better than the rest. But you, Lord, turn to us and have pity.

C: *Lord, you know everything; you know that we love you.*

L: Lord, we have often belittled the needy instead of giving them our help. But you, Lord, turn to us and have pity.

C: *Lord, you know everything; you know that we love you.*

L: We have often been unfaithful to the gifts of the Spirit in our communities. But you, Lord, turn to us and have pity.

C: *Lord, you know everything; you know that we love you.*

L: Let us pray that God may forgive our faults, especially those which have separated us from our fellow Christians and have provoked or maintained divisions among us.

Here the members of the congregation may add prayers for forgiveness, reconciliation, and unity.

Speaker: We know that God is full of mercy and forgives us when we ask sincerely for forgiveness. Because we are loved and forgiven, we also love and forgive one another. Therefore, let us show one another a sign of peace.

(exchange of the sign of peace)

The 1980s

This decade, marked in Canada by the Quebec referendum (1980) and internationally by the fall of the Berlin Wall (1989), was one of intense questioning. The following text was featured on the cover of the 1980 Week of Prayer Canadian resources:

Either: The people of God will remain fragmented in a multitude of splinter groups, mutually opposed or indifferent, incapable of sharing the joys and sufferings of the entire human family. Then it will not be surprising that the men and women of our time turn from the Church in ever greater numbers, and that she is replaced by indifference or by the ideologies of an imposed sharing.

Or: Christians, rooted in the celebration of Christ dead and risen, will enter upon a process of reconciliation, rediscover a visible communion around a universal pastor, and widen their solidarity to include every human being. It will be Springtime: The Church will become what she is, seed of a new humanity, reconciled at last.

(*The Acts of the Council of Youth, Taizé, France*)

This stark, realistic-hopeful expression speaks to one of the strong themes to emerge during Prayer for Christian Unity in this decade. In North America this was the time of Reaganomics, Yuppies, a growing technocracy, Music Television, and a rapid economic boom and bust. In the midst of these various kingdoms, the churches asked, "What does it mean to pray '*Your* kingdom come'"? For Christians, it means choosing hope and following values above the competition of the culture; it means solidarity with the victims of the powers of society; it means waking up to the fact that ecumenism is an essential part of living the Gospel.

Through the now much-expanded Week of Prayer for Christian Unity resources, the Joint Working Group of the Canadian Conference of Catholic Bishops and the Canadian Council of Churches articulated a common vision of ecumenism. They asked: What are we praying? We are praying the prayer of Christ. Why is there an ecumenical movement? The 1980 Week of Prayer booklet says, "Precisely because of the need to make baptized believers of all denominations aware that when we maintain our centuries-old divisions or when we create new ones, we are betraying Jesus Christ." To grasp truly what it means to pray as Jesus taught is to see that ecumenism is not an "add on" to what it means to be a Christian. Nor is it simply an efficient tool for cooperation in mission, service and advocacy. It is a *must*.

Resource booklets, now published by Novalis, were larger and included plenty of educational materials to help local communities to learn from each other and to learn about the work that the churches in Canada were doing together. The churches were learning, through advocacy and solidarity work in relation to South Africa and Latin America, for example, that "solidarity is life." In the Week of Prayer, Christians were invited into the powerful experience of holding each other in prayer around the world. A new tradition had begun: each year an ecumenical group from a particular country wrote the text; this was then shared with the world. Local communities adapted and expanded the materials as needed. The Canadian version now made sure to include a reflection and information about the country that had developed the text in order to nurture a prayerful solidarity and learning with that community. The Canadian interpretation of the themes within this decade shows attention to the value of unity within diversity, celebrating the particularity of uniqueness of cultures and languages within the household of God. Jesus Christ is the life of the world, sings the 1983 theme, which was also adopted as the theme of that year's World Council of Churches Assembly in Vancouver. Life – in its *liveliness* – consists of many lives; their language and culture and expression of faith are all drawn together in Christ.

Celebration of diversity and the necessity of solidarity thus became two key themes within this decade, as the Joint Working Group sought to use the opportunity of the Week of Prayer for Christian Unity to develop a self-consciously Canadian expression of the ecumenical vision, and so address the more negative powers of the dominant culture. The message in the 1989 Week of Prayer for Christian Unity kit is unequivocal:

> "Lonely in a crowd" is more than an empty phrase today. In our panic for security, we not only keep intruders out but we lock ourselves in. Apart from one another, our circle can become so small that we are isolated from valuable social and spiritual contacts. We need these to grow, to develop into the people of God. As we relate to others, we find ourselves drawing upon one another's gifts and abilities. None of us can be fully self-sufficient … The apostle Paul compared the relationship of one member to another within the Christian community to the different parts of the human body which depend upon one another for their very existence. In Canadian society we encounter a wonderful variety of languages, cultures and religious traditions. We sometimes hear it described as a mosaic, where each piece remains distinct, yet contributes to the whole, rather than a melting pot in which individual identities are lost. The "stew pot" may be an even better image for the kind of Christian community we are seeking during this Week of Prayer for Christian Unity. As we join together in worship we bring the flavours, colours and textures of the Christian traditions from which we come. We do not lose our distinctiveness, but neither do we remain unchanged. Each is enhanced and enriched by sharing with others in the Body of Christ. Together with Christ and with one another we have a rich flavour that we could never have apart.

J.E. Scully

The Great Milestones in Our March Towards Christian Unity

Canadian Council of Churches / Canadian Conference of Catholic Bishops (1980)

1910 – World Missionary Conference at Edinburgh: Christians must witness with one voice to the Good News of Salvation.

1948 – Founding, in Amsterdam, of the World Council of Churches: Christians act in concert at the world level.

1960 – John XXIII creates the Secretariat for Promoting Christian Unity; with Vatican II, the Roman Catholic Church enters fully into the ecumenical movement.

1964 – Paul VI meets with the Orthodox patriarch Athenagoras in Jerusalem; mutual excommunications existing since 1054 are removed.

1966 – Paul VI meets with Dr. Ramsey, primate of the Anglican Communion; a dialogue is opened between "two sister Churches."

Must Christians Work Together for Justice?

Canadian Council of Churches / Canadian Conference of Catholic Bishops (1980)

The Lund principle: "We must act jointly in all things, except where differences in our convictions force us to act separately." Such was the principle laid down by the Churches meeting in the Faith and Order Assembly, in Lund, Sweden, in 1952. It is in this spirit that the Churches of the world are committing themselves more and more to speaking out with a single voice on social, economic and political issues, through groups and agencies financed, staffed and operated by several Churches acting in common.

On the international level, among the best-known of these organizations are SODEPAX, for social development and peace, and Amnesty International, which assists in the liberation of political prisoners, the Inter-Church Aid, Refugee and World Service of the World Council of Churches.

In Canada, there are more than fifty such interdenominational groups, including PLURA, which was created to promote social justice in our country and invests over $200,000 a year in the struggle against poverty; GATT-Fly, an action-research group working on problems of global economic justice including the impact of Canadian trade policies on Third World countries; the Inter-Church Committee on Human Rights in Latin America, which is responsible for education and action on the repression of human rights in various Latin American countries today; Project-North, which had undertaken a program of study and action on ethical issues underlying Northern development and its impact on native peoples; Ten Days For World Development, which sponsors an annual public education campaign on world development, such as the problems of world hunger; the Task Force on Churches and Corporate Responsibility, which coordinates research in various aspects of the moral responsibility of multinational corporations.

Your Kingdom Come!
(Graymoor, 1980)

We pray "Your Kingdom come"
    for the greater honour of God, as did the psalmist (Psalm 95, 97, 99);
    for the welfare of all men, women, and children (John 10:10);
    for the redeeming of creation (Romans 8:19);
    for the coming of the unity of all in the one Kingdom (Revelations 21:3).

The Peace – A Supplication
Canadian Council of Churches (1981)

Send on us and all people, the peace Jesus gives:
    the peace which the world cannot give,
    which we cannot find in ourselves;
    the peace which unites us to God;
    the peace which unites us with one another;
    the peace which gives healing within.

God's peace be with us all!
May this peace enable us to recognize your truth in our different traditions.
May this lead us to accept one another, for we have received the same Spirit.

Service of Prayer for Christian Unity

Graymoor (1981)

Hymn

Welcome

Leader: Grace and peace to you from God our Father and from the Lord Jesus Christ. (Ephesians 1:2)

Congregation: *Blessed be God the Father of our Lord Jesus Christ, who has blessed us with all the spiritual blessings of heaven in Christ.* (Ephesians 1:3)

L: O Source of Life, whose will it is that your people should be one in love and in truth, renew in your church the gift of your Spirit of holiness. May we be filled with the diversity of your gifts and be guided along the ways you choose toward the fullness of unity. We ask this in the name of Jesus Christ, who lives now and forever.

C: *Amen.*

Psalm / Hymn

I Reading: 1 Corinthians 12:3b-13

Response: *Yours, Lord Jesus, be the glory and the praise.*

II Reading: John 16:12-15

Response: *Yours, Lord Jesus, be the glory and the praise.*

Homily / Address

At the conclusion of the homily/address, the congregation will be invited to contribute to a collection on behalf of the special needs of some joint Christian project, as a sign of renewed Christian fellowship.

A Litany of Unity

L: Blessed are you, O Lord, our God, for you enable us through your Holy Spirit to confess that Jesus Christ is Lord.

C: *We thank you, O God.*

L: For there are varieties of gifts, but the same Spirit.

C: *We thank you, O God.*

L: For there are varieties of service, but the same Lord.

C: *We thank you, O God.*

L: For it is the same God who is working in us all.

C: *We thank you, O God.*

L: For to each of us the Spirit gives all gifts for the common good.

C: *We thank you, O God.*

L: We seek, O Lord, the gifts of your Holy Spirit. We seek the ability to explore the depths of truth and share what we find with others.

C: *May we grow in the likeness of Christ.*

L: We seek the gift of faith which supports our hopes and leads us to the One Source of all life.

C: *May we grow into the likeness of Christ.*

L: We seek the grace to heal our divisions.

C: *May we grow into the likeness of Christ.*

L: We seek the light to discern your activity in the world and to proclaim your love and justice for all.

C: *May we grow into the likeness of Christ.*

L: We seek the praise which can lift our spirits and can enliven our worship.

C: *May we grow into the likeness of Christ.*

L: Your gifts, O Lord, are ours to share, and so we pray for others: For those whose lives of loving faith and service have led others to work for reconciliation, we pray:

C: *Lord, have mercy.*

L: For the sick, the suffering, the captive; for their safety and emancipation, we pray:

C: *Lord, have mercy.*

L: For those who proclaim God's will for the church and for the world, we pray:

C: *Lord, have mercy.*

L: Let us join our prayers and say:

C: *Our Father …*

L: We ask you, O God,
   to forgive our sins,
   to forgive us because we are still separated,
   to forgive us because we do not reflect your liberating love to the whole world.
   Teach us to overcome our divisions.
   Send us your Holy Spirit to guide us into the fullness of truth.
   We stand before you with our partial understandings,
   with traditions we have developed over the centuries,
   with new insights we have recently been given.
   Grant us your peace, the peace that comes from you through Jesus Christ,
   the peace that the world cannot give,
   the peace that we cannot find ourselves.
   May your peace be with us.
   May we recognize the truth that is present in our different traditions.
   May we accept one another as sisters and brothers
   who have received the same Holy Spirit.

Greetings of Peace

L: We have been blessed by God with the gift of Jesus Christ, the Lord,
   who is our peace.
   In him we give you thanks and praise, O God.
   All gifts are from you.
   You call us your people and ask us to be faithful stewards.
   May we always realize your loving care.
   May hymns of praise and thanksgiving rise from our hearts,
   inspired by one and the same Holy Spirit.

C: *Amen.*

Dismissal

L: Let us lift our voices in common prayer of praise.

C: *Praise God in his temple on earth*
   Praise God in his temple of heaven;
   Praise God for his mighty works;
   Praise God's almighty goodness!
   Praise God with blasts of the trumpet;
   Praise God with lyre and harp;
   Praise God with drums and dancing;
   Praise God with strings and reeds;
   Praise God with clashing cymbals;

Praise God with clanging cymbals!
Let everything that breathes praise God!

L: May God bless you and keep you.
May God's face shine upon you and be gracious to you.
May God grant you peace.

C: *Amen. Praise God!*

May All Find Their Home in You

Canadian Council of Churches (1982)

Leader: Great is, O King, our happiness in your kingdom, you our king.

People: *May all find their home in you.*

L: We dance before you, our king, by the strength of your kingdom.

P: *May all find their home in you.*

L: May our feet be made strong; let us dance before you, Eternal One.

P: *May all find their home in you.*

L: Give praise, all you angels, to him above who is worthy of all praise.

P: *May all find their home in you.*

L: For the Churches, throughout the world, that we may all be one, let us pray:

P: *May all find their home in you.*

L: For the world we live in, that all may enjoy peace, justice and freedom, let us pray:

P: *May all find their home in you.*

L: For our community, that it may have a welcome for all, let us pray:

P: *May all find their home in you.*

L: For the needy, for the homeless, for refugees – let us pray:

P: *May all find their home in you.*

L: For the sick, the suffering, the captive; for their safety and salvation, let us pray:

P: *May all find their home in you.*

L: For our families, our friends, and all here present, let us pray:

P: *May all find their home in you.*

L: For all we remember in love, let us pray:

P: *May all find their home in you.*

Rite of Conclusion

O God, you have let us pass the day in peace; let us pass the night in peace. O Lord, you have no Lord. There is no strength but in you. There is no unity but in your house. Under your hand we pass the night. You are our mother and our father. You are our home. Amen. *(from the Boran of Kenya)*

Jesus Christ – The Life of the World
(Canadian Council of Churches, 1983)

Some years ago a question chalked on the hoardings of a damaged city in Northern Ireland caught the eye of international reporters. It asked, "Is there life before death?" We can understand the horror and even the despair behind that inversion of a common theme. What we may not understand, perhaps, is the determined celebration of life, despite surrounding death, which characterizes many people in Northern Ireland. There, and in other countries of the world where the results of personal and social sin may appear more vicious than in our own, abundant life is manifest. It is life which has its source in a faith animating thsoe communities of believers to give common witness to peace, justice and compassion.

The theme of the 1983 Week of Prayer for Christian Unity celebrates Jesus, as a special manifestation of life in our world. Through his example on earth of preaching, teaching, healing and building a community of believers, he made eternal life visible in a new way. Through his death and resurrection he made it possible for us to share that life and to proclaim it in the world. United to him through the power of the Holy Spirit we can face death and evil knowing that they are not finally triumphant.

As in Jesus' time in history, so in ours, life is threatened on many fronts. The more obvious threats are war, famine, selfish and oppressive systems, lack of meaning, loneliness… We know, too, that as individuals and as churches we are divided by sin and history, and that the darkness of death has not left us untouched. And yet we know that we are constantly drawn by the Holy Spirit into deeper communion with God and with one another – to pray, to break bread, to live in love and service, and to proclaim the good news that Jesus lives.

If Christ's life is to flow through us to a world which desperately needs our caring, our struggles for peace and justice, our knowledge and experience of God's forgiving and healing love, we must pray and act *together*. If Christ's prayer for unity that the world may believe and find life in abundance is to bear fruit, the churches must, more than ever, witness to the life of Jesus active in our lives and in our communities.

Day 6: Life is proclaimed to the world

Isaiah 61:1-4; Psalm 34 (33):1-10; II Corinthians 4:7-15; Matthew 28:16-20

Isaiah tells of the coming from God of one who will bring good news to the afflicted, will bind the brokenhearted, proclaim liberty to the captives and comfort all who mourn. Christians see in Jesus the fulfillment of Isaiah's promise. It was this passage that Jesus used to refer to his ministry when he spoke in the synagogue at Nazareth. Christians are sent into the world to witness, by what they say and do, to their hope and faith.

For reflection: Whom can we identify as the afflicted and brokenhearted in our day?
In what ways can we embody Christ's ministry to them?

Prayer (from Northern Ireland)

Leader: Father God, we are people of our time and of our situation. Around us are the signs and symbols of fear, of hatred, of death. Father, we have tried to find ways to peace and reconciliation, but always too little, always too late, always our hopes have been destroyed. We are perplexed and angry and, even, hopeless. We want to walk away from it all, to wash our hands of it, to get out.

But every time we turn to go, our way is blocked, barred by a cross, the cross of Christ. You, Lord, make us people of hope. You save us from cynicism and despair. You give us hope founded on your victory over evil, over hatred, even over death itself. And his hope in your risen life breaks into our broken life as a light shining out of deep darkness, as a seed growing even in a wasteland.

Father, we are people of our time. All around us are signs of despair, yet we hope in the sign of signs – your empty cross. For you are alive for ever more and your people are prisoners – prisoners of hope.

People: *Thanks be to God. Amen.*

We Arise Today

Canadian Council of Churches (1983)

We arise today
Through a mighty strength,
the invocation of the Trinity,
Through belief in the threeness,

Through confession of the oneness
Of the Creator of Creation.

(adaptation of a traditional Irish prayer ascribed to Saint Patrick)

Commitment to Unity

Canadian Council of Churches (1984)

We accept anew our call to make visible our unity in Christ.
We pledge ourselves to serve one another in love,
not only by words but by deeds.
With God's help, we will strengthen our efforts for common action
and prayer during this year.

Mother Teresa's Daily Prayer

Graymoor (1984)

The congregation repeats each line after the leader.

Leader: Make us worthy, Lord,
to serve our sisters well.
Make us worthy, Lord,
to serve our brothers well
throughout the world who live and die
In poverty and hunger.

Give them, through our hands,
this day, their daily bread
Give them, through our hands,

this day, their daily bread
And by our understanding love
Give peace and joy.

O Christ, in Your Resurrection

Canadian Council of Churches (1985)

Resurrection

Leader: O Christ, in your resurrection you have destroyed death.

All: *Alleluia*

L: O Christ, in your resurrection you have brought all humanity from death to life.

All: *Alleluia*

L: O Christ, in your resurrection you spoke joyful news
to the women and the apostles, and salvation for the whole world.

All: *Alleluia*

L: O Christ, in your resurrection you breathed the Holy Spirit upon your disciples.

All: *Alleluia*

L: O Christ, in your resurrection you promised to be with us to the end of time.

All: *Alleluia*

L: O Christ, in your resurrection you sent your apostles to the ends of the earth.

All: *Alleluia*

L: O Christ, in your resurrection you are the beginning,
the Firstborn from among the dead.

All: *Alleluia*

L: O Christ, in your resurrection you reconcile all things on earth and in heaven.

All: *Alleluia*

Reconciliation

Leader: Across the barriers that divide Christians:

All: *Reconcile us, O Christ.*

L: Across the barriers that divide race from race:

All: *Reconcile us, O Christ.*

L: Across the barriers that divide the rich from the poor:

All: *Reconcile us, O Christ.*

L: Across the barriers that divide people of different faiths:

All: *Reconcile us, O Christ.*

L: Across the barriers that divide men and women, young and old:

All: *Reconcile us, O Christ.*

Leader: Confront us, O Christ, with the hidden prejudices and fears which deny and betray our prayers. Enable us to see the cause of strife; remove from us all false sense of superiority. Teach us to grow in unity with all God's children. Amen.

(adapted from the World Council of Churches Vancouver Worship Book)

O Christ, Radiant Light

Graymoor (1985)

Leader: O Christ, radiant Light, shining in our darkness,
you are the most glorious of the children of humankind,
the only Holy One among us sinners,
the Source of Life who have sanctified our mortal nature:

All: *Son of the Living God, save us all!*

L: You stooped low and humbled yourself. You became obedient unto death.
You walked the sorrowful road to the cross,
and you call us to follow you in every moment of our lives,
to death with you and to resurrection with you:

All: *Son of the Living God, save us all!*

L: You have saved us in our poverty and won justification for us,
to make us a holy nation, a People of kings and priests to God your Father:

All: *Son of the Living God, save us all!*

L: You grant us all the fullness of your Grace through the gift of the Holy Spirit.
Risen Lord, save us from death: Living Lord, make us sharers in your life.
Conqueror, give us your victory!

All: *Son of the Living God, save us all!*

L: Burn in us all that is not kindled by your presence,
and break in us all that would rebel against you,
that hearts may be fully your own as we wait for the day of your revelation,
when we shall be like you as we see you face to face.

All: *Son of the Living God, save us all!*

(from the Taizé Prayer Book)

Your Will Be Done

Canadian Council of Churches (1986)

Leader: Let us pray for the gift of unity.

Silent prayer.

L: God, our Father, who has created all things, we are your children.
It is your will that we live together in peace and stand by one another
as sisters and brothers.

All: *Your will be done.*

L: Jesus Christ, Son of God, you have prayed for the unity of all who are baptized
in your name, who believe in you and confess your name.
It is your will that the church, your body, be one.

All: *Your will be done.*

L: Holy Spirit of God, You filled the Apostles with the fire of courage
to proclaim the Good News. It is your will that we proclaim with one voice
the great deeds of God and the Good News of Jesus Christ.

All: *Your will be done.*

L: Let us pray for the world.

Silent prayer

O God, Creator of all things,
From you we receive our life.
You have blessed us with the gifts
of your creation in endless fullness.
Help us to be responsible stewards of your creation;
to protect life where it is in danger
and to heal life where it is broken.

All: *Grant this, O Lord.*

L. Gracious God, you gave your Son that we may have life and that no one be lost.
Let your love come to light in us and in the churches,
that your gospel may be heard in the world
and that people may find fulfillment in you.

All: *Grant this, O Lord.*

Leader: Let us pray for peace.

Silent prayer

Lord, our God, you are a God of peace.
In your Son Jesus Christ you have brought into the world the Word of reconciliation
and you have called us to be peacemakers.
We pray for those who are victims of wars and oppression,
for those whose rights and human dignity are denied,
for those who are persecuted because of their beliefs.
We pray for those who have to suffer under hatred and injustice.

All: *Hear our prayer, O Lord.*

L: Give to the church here and everywhere
   the courage to speak your name where peace is threatened
   and violence dominates the human condition.
   Give us the strength to make visible your reconciling love in our everyday life.

All: *Hear our prayer, O Lord.*

L: Let us pray for the witness of Christians in this community.

Silent prayer

Gracious God, you have granted to us communion with yourself
by uniting us to Christ and to one another.
As people belonging to different branches of your church,
teach us to value the diverse gifts of grace and truth you have given to each.

All: *Lord, in your mercy, hear our prayer.*

L: Deliver us from misunderstanding, prejudice and self-righteousness.

All: *Lord, in your mercy, hear our prayer.*

L: Keep us faithful in our commitment and witness,
   so that the world may believe in One Lord,
   who is the Way, the Truth and the Life.

All: *Lord, in your mercy, hear our prayer.*

Penitential Rite

Graymoor (1986)

Leader: Before we can witness together we must repent of our divisions
        and seek mutual pardon of each other.
        Lord, we have sinned against you and against our sisters and brothers.

All: *Lord, have mercy.*

L: O Christ, our divisions are contrary to your will,
and have impeded our common witness to you.

All: *Lord, have mercy.*

L: Lord, we have not loved you enough in our brothers and sisters,
created in your image, but different from us.

A: *Lord, have mercy.*

L: May the Lord have mercy on us, forgive us our sins and bring us to everlasting life.

A: *Amen.*

L: In the name of all those who search for a more complete unity among Christians,
who pray and work for this goal, let us exchange a sign of peace in the Spirit of Christ,
as a symbol of mutual reconciliation, of growing unity and of love.
Let us extend a greeting of reconciliation and peace to one another.

"You Shall Be My Witnesses"

Graymoor (1986)

When the Lord Jesus said farewell to his disciples, he told them: "You will receive power when the Holy Spirit has come upon you; and you shall be my witnesses in Jerusalem and in all Judea and Samaria and to the ends of the earth" (Acts 1:8). With these words Our Lord sent them and his disciples of all generations among men and women in every time and place, to witness the power behind his words and the hope his message offers the world. He intends this power and this hope to flow into the human community in its fidelity to his words and works. This year's Week of Prayer for Christian Unity is observed under this theme: You Shall Be My Witnesses.

Last year's Week of Prayer observance was under the theme: *From Death to Life with Christ*. This year's theme continues that of last year by its emphasis on the responsibility of Christians to bring their prayer into the realm of action. As a week of prayer, really an octave of prayer, we have an opportunity to open the Christian community in a very special way to the grace of God. People need to be encouraged, to be delivered from quiet despair and strident cynicism. Under the grace of God we move from the activity of prayer to a protest over what is happening in our world and our American society. "To protest" is another way of "witnessing on behalf of." To protest can be something very positive and affirmative.

And so we can protest a technological mentality that challenges deeper human values. We witness on behalf of Christ when we ask critical questions and affirm basic moral principles as one community of faith; when we protest a technology that easily affirms that whatever we learn to control and manipulate in human life is automatically valid and allowable.

The issues of life and death on our planet are still very much with us. Anxiety over nuclear destruction, the decisions on who lives or dies in the womb or the ward, life above and below the poverty line, billions for defense and a pittance for justice — all these make demands on the individual Christian conscience. We cannot expect a Christian consensus in all the bewildering complexity that is forced on us. But we pray for a new vision that will help us find a coherent approach to these problems. Such coherence demands an authentic concern for all our sisters and brothers. It will not be given us apart from prayer. We need to raise our hearts as well as our consciousness. We need to pray that power in the Spirit and hope in God's promises will be given in such abundance that the powerless and despairing draw real strength from the Christian presence in our American society.

In light of all this we can speak to the need for a common witness. We have been divided not only at the level of doctrine, but at the level of life and witness. It is true we have a common heritage in the One Lord, One Faith, One Baptism. Our common apostolic faith is expressed in the Bible and ancient creeds. Baptism brings us together in Christ as the Body of Christ. But while we do not want to impose a single mind-set, we do look for a more normal coordination in the Body of Christ.

The need for such coordination and common witness has inspired the Christian unity movement. There is evidence that such coordination and common witness is growing in local church life, in social concerns, and in theological dialogue. In American life in particular, there seems to be a new context for united Christian witness, while allowing diversity and difference. A 1980 document coming from a Joint Working Group of the Roman Catholic Church and the World Council of Churches states:

> In a world where there is confusion, where many people seem uncertain, the search for unity and a common witness is an act and sign of hope.

It is in the power of God's Spirit, with the desire to share our hope with others, that we celebrate this 1986 Week of Prayer under the Lord's injunction: You Shall Be My Witnesses.

Give Us Your Holy Spirit

Graymoor (1988)

Leader: Make us one, O God, in our eagerness to speak good news
    and set all captives free.

People: *Give us your Holy Spirit.*

L: Make us one, O God, in concern for the poor, the hurt, and the downtrodden,
    to show them your love.

P: *Give us your Holy Spirit.*

L: Make us one, O God, in worship, breaking bread together and singing your praise
with single voice.

P: *Give us your Holy Spirit.*

L: Make us one, O God, in faithfulness to Jesus Christ, who never fails us,
and who will come again in triumph.

P: *Give us your Holy Spirit.*

L: Give us your Holy Spirit, O God, so we may have among us
the same mind that was in Christ Jesus and proclaim him to the world.
May every knee bow down and every tongue confess him Lord,
to the glory of your name.

P: *Amen.*

L: As Christ sent disciples into every land, O God, gather them now,
from the ends of the earth, into one fellowship that chooses your purpose
and praises your name, in one faith, one hope, and one love that casts out fear.

P: *Amen.*

A Profession of Faith

Canadian Council of Churches (1988)

All: Lord, you have always given bread for the coming day,
and though I am poor, today I believe.
Lord, you have always given strength for the coming day,
and though I am weak, today I believe.
Lord, you have always given peace for the coming day,
and though of anxious heart, today I believe.
Lord, you have always kept me safe in trials,
and though I now am tried, today I believe.
Lord, you have always marked the road for the coming day,
and though it may be hid, today I believe.
Lord, you have always lit this darkness of mine,
and though the night is here, today I believe.
Lord, you have always spoken when the time was right,
and despite your silence now, today I believe.

Your Church Is Like a Mosaic

Graymoor (1989)

Leader: Lord, you bless those who praise you
and sanctify those who put their trust in you;
save your people and bless your inheritance.
Protect the whole body of your Church.
Sanctify those who love the beauty of your house,
glorify them with your divine power
and do not forsake those who put their hope in you.

All: *God, your Church is like a mosaic of pieces, large and small,*
of many colors and shapes, whose differences, when blended,
make a thing of beauty not possible for any piece alone.
Help us to be trusting as you bring us together.
Grant us the grace to regard our neighbors with genuine love,
knowing that however ill-matched we feel,
we may become a perfect fit to you – who can see the whole picture.
For every good and perfect gift comes from above,
from you the Father of lights; and to you we give glory, thanksgiving and worship,
to the Father, and to the Son, and to the Holy Spirit,
now and forever, to the ages of ages. Amen.

Benediction

Canadian Council of Churches (1989)

Leader: You who are called by God to build the Christian community,
be the light of the world.
In your every word and every deed let Jesus reach out to others in love.

All: *Alleluia, alleluia, amen!*

L: Be servants of your sisters and brothers in giving food and drink,
clothing and shelter, in visiting them in their need.

All: *Alleluia, alleluia, amen!*

L: Be one in Christ, and go forth so that in meeting you
the world may know the love of God.

All: *Alleluia, alleluia, amen!*

L: May the blessing of the Lord, through his divine grace and love,
rest upon you now and forever, to the ages of ages.

All: *Amen.*

The 1990s

During this decade, the Canadian Week of Prayer for Christian Unity kits were greatly expanded. The links between prayer and bible study had been part of the Week of Prayer movement from the beginning, but a particular passion of the Canadian writing team, in adapting the international materials, was to make a point about the many other ways in which ecumenism is nurtured and expressed. Thematic material, worship services, biblical reflections, exegetical commentaries, homiletic suggestions and prayers were woven together with a wide range of adult educational resources, materials for children and youth, and a growing suggested activities section emphasizing mutual education and co-operation in justice and peace work. More than ever, the Week of Prayer was reaching for a broader understanding of ecumenism: that unity in the Body of Christ is about the wideness of God's embrace, and therefore touches and informs all of what we do.

Along with this holistic approach is found a mystic element, re-emphasizing that prayer is the soul of the ecumenical movement and that the prayer that all may be one is the prayer of Christ, into which we enter. During a decade in which the word "downsizing" was added to the Oxford English Dictionary, and was known within the organizational structures of churches themselves, a reassertion of fierce, individualistic competitiveness was visible. And yet the churches were involved in commitments of solidarity ecumenically – in the Ecumenical Decade of Churches in Solidarity with Women, and in the hearings of the Royal Commission on Aboriginal Peoples, for example. Amid this work, the Week of Prayer was an opportunity for the churches together to do some teaching about prayer itself.

"In our time and society, prayer is commonly seen as a way of getting our own way. Sports teams and political parties pray for victory. ... We practice 'gimme prayers'," proclaimed the 1991 Week of Prayer resource. To counter-balance this view of prayer, the decade's Week of Prayer materials emphasized the ways of entering into a deeper sense of mutual belonging, in Christ and in each other, in and through our prayer. Christians were called to learn each other's "languages," traditions and ways of doing things the better to be enriched. Much care was taken to explain the religious and cultural traditions and contexts behind the worship services offered each year, and to invite Christians into forms of prayer that might be different from those of their own traditions and cultures. This type of prayer invites people to move outside of themselves and enhances a sense of mutual belonging that does not erase distinctivenesses for the sake of unity, but brings unity to expression through the promise of mutual "in-dwelling" of persons in Christ. This view of prayer is built explicitly on a Trinitarian mysticism, a major theological cornerstone throughout this decade.

Ecumenism itself underwent a significant shift during this time: no longer did it imply union, but rather mutual understanding and acceptance. The sense of belonging was being developed self-consciously within the organizational self-understanding of the Canadian Council of Churches. The late 1990s saw the change in the Canadian Council of Churches self-consciously to structure its life and work explicitly as a forum of churches as distinct, for example, from an agency of or for the churches. The point was to make sure that the churches *as churches* were coming together within the Council, fully representative and participatory from their own traditions and individual ecclesial structures. This move enabled the Canadian Conference of Catholic Bishops to become full members of the Canadian Council of Churches in 1997, along with the Christian Reformed Church of Canada soon after.

One can read the Week of Prayer resources as an expression of the theology leading up to and then explicitly giving voice to this "forum" notion. We are called to *live by the Spirit* (1993) and are thereby reminded that God's love bears fruit in a large variety of ways. In the years that followed, reflections on being in the household of God and sharing in God's life bore out the self-consciously mystical-Trinitarian reflections on prayer and on our mutual in-dwelling both in Christ and in each other. We share in God's life, which is itself a distinctiveness of three Persons, and are called to share in each other's lives, which are also an expression of being in God's life. Reflecting on the theme of "Opening the Doors," the President of the Canadian Council of Churches in 1996 spoke of experiences within the work of the Council. At meetings, the churches' representatives on the Governing Board took time to open doors to each other, inviting them into the life, worship patterns and traditions of their particular churches. This experience was more than "getting to know you better," as important as that is. It was expressive of something much deeper, the reconciling presence of God in the midst of the churches.

J.E. Scully

Prayer of Repentance

Graymoor (1990)

Leader: Brothers and sisters, we place ourselves before God's word which reveals to us our responsibility for unity. That is why it leads us to ask for the Lord's forgiveness for our sins against unity. Lord, forgive our sinfulness.

All: *Lord, have mercy.*

L: For not celebrating humble confident prayer for unity; and for not keeping silent so that the Holy Spirit may implant in us the prayer of Jesus on the evening before his death, "that all may be one." Lord, forgive our sinfulness.

All: *Lord, have mercy.*

L: The Lord is merciful and gracious, slow to anger and abounding in steadfast love. Not always chiding; not remaining angry forever. God does not deal with us according to our sins, nor repay us according to our iniquities.

For this reason, I declare to you in the name of the Lord the forgiveness he brings to us.

All: *Amen.*

To God Be the Glory

Canadian Council of Churches (1990)

Leader: Let us now commit ourselves to be sanctified in truth.
Lord, we seek to know you, the one true God,
and Jesus Christ whom you have sent in the communion of the Holy Spirit
who leads us into truth.

All: *To God be the glory: Sanctify us in truth.*

L: To practise in our daily lives all we have received and learned in Jesus Christ, our Saviour.

All: *To God be the glory: Sanctify us in truth.*

L: To show forth his joy to the world in full measure.

All: *To God be the glory: Sanctify us in truth.*

L: That united in the prayer of Christ we may be one so that the world may believe.

All: *To God be the glory: Sanctify us in truth.*

L: Let us share the peace of Christ with one another.

The Challenge of Unity

Canadian Council of Churches (1991)

This year's Week of Prayer material was drafted early in 1989 by a West German ecumenical committee in consultation with the Pontifical Council for Promoting Christian Unity and the Faith and Order Commission of the World Council of Churches.

When a German drafting group was chosen almost two years ago nobody could have foreseen the dramatic events about to occur. In October and November 1989, a political renewal movement in East Germany culminated in the breaking down of the Berlin Wall and the beginning of a reunification process, a prospect which has been greeted with both hope and concern.

Removing barriers and reuniting peoples speaks to our Christian tradition which has always prayed for the unity of the Church. Yet, here too, the search for unity is not without ambiguity. There is enthusiasm and joy; there are difficulties, fears and disappointments.

Even as events in Germany symbolize new possibilities for human reconciliation, they challenge us to renewed efforts for increased understanding among, as well as within, nations, communities and families.

Praise the Lord, All You Nations!

Canadian Council of Churches (1991)

All: *Alleluia! Alleluia! Alleluia!*

Reading: Luke 1:46-55 or Luke 1:67-79

Response: *Laudate omnes gentes* (Taizé)

Homily

The homily may guide the congregation to a period of silent meditation on a slide or slides projected or on a picture reproduced for the order of service, if desired.

Response to the Homily

Leader: God, you are the source of all life. We praise your holy name!

All: *God, you are the source of all life.*

L: But very often we complain and do not feel satisfied with our life.

All: *God, you are the source of all life.*

L: Moans cross our lips easily, much more easily than praise and thanks.

All: *God, you are the source of all life. We praise your holy name!*

L: Forgive our faint-heartedness, Lord, and strengthen our faith.

All: *God, you are the source of all life. We praise your holy name!*

L: Forgive our selfishness, Lord, and let us be ever mindful that there is one God, and there is one mediator, Christ Jesus, who came as a ransom for all, to whom we testify.

All: *This saying is sure and worthy of full acceptance:*
　　that Jesus Christ came into the world to save sinners,
　　and was manifested in the flesh,
　　vindicated in the Spirit,
　　seen by angels,
　　proclaimed among the nations,
　　believed in throughout the world,
　　taken up in glory.
　　Great indeed is the mystery of the gospel. Amen.

　　(From 1 Timothy 2:5-6; 1:15; 3:16)

Leader: Let us share the peace of Christ with one another.

All may share a gesture or sign of peace. According to local custom this may be a handshake, kiss, bow or another sign.

Hymn or Special Music

The Blessing of the Bread

The blessing of the bread comes originally from the Orthodox Church, although there have been similar expressions in Catholic and Protestant traditions. It is not a celebration of the Eucharist, but a thanksgiving prayer for God's good creation.

Leader: Creator God, we bless and praise your name that all good gifts come from your hand. Seeds once scattered over fields have been gathered to become one in this bread. We pray that your people will be gathered from the borders of the earth that all may become one according to the prayer of your Son.

All: *As once he blessed the five loaves in the desert*
　　to feed the five thousand,
　　so now bless this bread,
　　and bless us as we share in a meal of love.
　　Grant that one day we may all be partakers at the heavenly table

where all glory and praise will be yours,
in unity with the Son and the Spirit in all eternity.

(Distribution of a common loaf or loaves in baskets. A song or hymn or other special music may be used while the bread is passed, or a time of silent reflection may accompany the act of sharing the loaves.)

Prayers of Intercession

Leader: God of wind and fire, let your spirit move among us that it may warm us and give us life. Already we glorify you together in prayer, songs of praise and hearing the Word. Lead us to take further steps towards the unity of all Christians. God, in your mercy,

All: *Hear our prayer.*

L: God of comfort, we praise your mercy, but in praising you, let us not forget the misery of the world, the fears of the weeping and despairing, the plight of the lonely and hurt, the desperation of those who have been tortured in body, soul and spirit. God, in your mercy,

All: *Hear our prayer.*

L: God of all the nations, let your church in the whole world draw new strength from worship and praise. Enable us to accept all peoples as you have accepted us. God, in your mercy,

All: *Hear our prayer.*

L: God of love, guide the church in the world, as it works for justice, prays for peace, and guards the integrity of creation. God, in your mercy,

All: *Hear our prayer.*

At this point, intercessions can be added in silence or in a free form of prayer.

L: God of grace, receive our prayers both spoken and silent; may they be in accordance with your will. Through Jesus Christ, with the guidance of your Holy Spirit, we pray;

All: *Our Father …*

Hymn

Blessing and Dismissal

Bread and Salt

Graymoor (1991)

Procession

Women, men and children, who represent participating congregations and a variety of ethnic backgrounds, carry a symbol which is a particular expression of faith or praise in their heritage. A large loaf of bread and a bowl of salt are also carried in procession. At the end of the hymn, the symbols are presented to the community:

I bring from the people of _____

this_____,

which symbolizes_____.

I bring this loaf of bread, a sign to all of us of our oneness in the body of Christ, the bread of life.

I bring this salt, a symbol of the integrity God has meant for us to embody.

Blessing of the Bread

Lord Jesus Christ, you blessed the five loaves of bread in the desert and fed the five thousand. Bless this bread, too, and make it holy as we distribute it amongst us. Just as this bread was once scattered over the fields and now is gathered up to become one loaf, so may your church be gathered from the borders of the earth. We pray that as a people of God we can overcome all divisions so that all who believe in you can share in the meal of your love. It is our hope that one day we shall all be guests at the eternal banquet prepared for all those who love God. Then shall all glory, adoration and praise be offered to you in unity with the Creator and the life-giving Spirit for all eternity. Amen.

Blessing of the Salt

Lord Jesus Christ, you have blessed us and called us to be the salt of the earth. Bless also this salt, a symbol of your mission in the world. Just as this salt is meant to season, so may we, through our lives, be the seasoning by which God's way is made visible in our communities and in our world. Amen.

Distribution of Bread and Salt

As we partake in this sharing of bread and salt, we pray that God will empower us to be the salt of the earth sharing together in the body of Christ so as to live and work for the realm of God, Creator, Redeemer and Sustainer, now and evermore.

The assembly is invited to take a piece of bread, dip it into the dish of salt and eat it.

Accept One Another, Just as Christ Accepted You

Canadian Council of Churches (1991)

Isaiah 61:8-11; Psalm 98; Revelation 19:4-9; Luke 15:1-10

The nations are arriving on our doorstep. Through immigration and tourism, through refuge granted to those in need, Canada has welcomed people of many cultures. Or are they welcome? Polls suggest that newcomers would be more welcome if they adopted the customs of the majority, eliminating differences. Yet Isaiah pictures God's welcome as a groom greeting a bride. We know that healthy marriages do not destroy the partners' diversity, but rejoice in mutuality shared within this diversity. As God has welcomed us in our global diversity, let us welcome one another as God's wedding guests and rejoice that God takes pleasure in us all.

Let us pray for the grace to welcome those who are different from us and to rejoice together in the unity we share as God's people.

"Make Disciples of All Nations…"

Canadian Council of Churches (1992)

Micah 6:6-8; Psalm 19:7-14; Galatians 5:22–6:2; John 15:8-17

"Discipline" calls to mind parental chastisement, curfews and other resented restrictions. The word "disciple," however, touches the core of discipline, which is learning. In Scripture, this learning circles around love — learning to love, learning in love, learning from love. Jesus abandoned the parental framework in his words about discipleship, choosing instead to speak of friendship. Disciples are friends who share knowledge and express mutual care out of a bond of love. To make disciples, then, asks us to make friends. Sharing the Gospel is not simply teaching the content of Scripture or rules of faith. It requires a discipline of the fruit of the Spirit to flavour our lives with love.

Pray that Christians of different traditions will make new friendships in Christ and flavour the world with God's love.

Remember Us in Your Kingdom

Graymoor (1992)

Leader: Lord Jesus Christ, by your death and resurrection you came into the glory of your Father. You go before us into the kingdom.

All: *And we sinners beg you: remember us in Your Kingdom.*

L: We pray for your Church throughout the whole world and for all who confess their faith in you. Help us draw nearer to you and come to know the unity which awaits us in you.

All: *And remember us in Your Kingdom.*

L: We pray for all those who proclaim your gospel in the nations and for those who bear witness to your truth before those who do not know you. You are their only Lord, as there is but one faith and one baptism. Go before them and be their only true hope.

All: *Remember them, Lord, in Your Kingdom.*

L: We pray for the victims of violence and injustice in this world of sin and division, for those who are at the edge of despair and for those who see the glow of hope on the horizon. Be with them in their suffering, Lord, who gave your life that men and women may be saved. And be with us, too, as we grow aware of our responsibility towards them and towards your world.

All: *Remember them and us in Your Kingdom.*

L: We pray for all the nations and for all peoples. Your kingdom is righteousness, peace and joy. Grant us the joy in the Spirit to be peacemakers among nations and to strive for true justice among all races and peoples.

All: *Remember them and us in Your Kingdom.*

L: Lord, hear our prayer for your Church and for the world. Soothe the sufferings of the unfortunate and bring them joy. Strengthen our resolve to preach your word to the world and to welcome the peace, the reconciliation and the unity which you came to proclaim. Be with us, Lord, always, to the end of the world.

All: *Amen.*

Invocation of the Holy Spirit

Graymoor (1993)

O Heavenly King, Comforter, Spirit of truth.
Present in all places and filling all things;
treasury of blessings and giver of life;
come and dwell in us.
Cleanse us from every impurity,
and of your goodness save our souls.

(from the Orthodox liturgy)

Guided by the Spirit

Canadian Council of Churches (1993)

The prayers may be offered by one or several leaders. A suitable silence may precede each response.

Leader: Gracious God,
   you sent your son, Jesus Christ,
   to gather all humanity into one family of believers,
   living in the law of liberty.
   In the power of your Spirit
   guide us to become custodians of your creation.

Silence may be kept

L: We pray,

People: *May we live and be guided by the Spirit.*

L: You have rescued us from the realm of darkness,
   you have brought us into the reign of light.
   Hasten the day when your whole creation,
   freed from slavery and oppression,
   will know the freedom and glory of your children.

Silence may be kept

L: We pray,

P: *May we live and be guided by the Spirit.*

L: Pour out your blessing on the whole creation;
    gather your church together in unity
    to proclaim your message of hope for the world.

Silence may be kept

L: We pray,

P: *May we live and be guided by the Spirit.*

L: O God, the bond of all affections,
    give us your Spirit of perfect unity,
    and transform us into a new humanity,
    free and united in your love.

Silence may be kept

L: We pray,

P: *May we live and be guided by the Spirit.*

Opening the Doors

Canadian Council of Churches (1994)

The following is a suggested format for an evening event (7:00–9:30 p.m.) that brings together young people of different churches in your community. The event is designed to be one way for participants to meet young people of other Christian traditions and be exposed to some of their traditions. Make the evening "an ecumenical event"! You may have other ideas that are more appropriate for your group. Use them! Be creative! This process is simply a guide.

A "Progressive" event

In many Canadian communities, churches of different denominations are often just around the corner from each other, or at most a short drive away. Though we may be neighbours, not all of us have spent much time within each other's houses of worship. This event is a chance to open the doors literally to each other. It will work best if the groups hosting the evening are close together, so that participants can walk or drive together in no more than ten minutes.

Begin with a tour

Many of us take first-time guests to our homes on a short tour. The "inside look" into one's living space can give a deepened appreciation of the host(s). "Opening the doors" to each other for this event means giving neighbours and friends an inside look at our worship space. The event has two main parts, each of which begins with a tour;

- a gathering time for participants to meet each other and begin to interact through one or two activities; and

- a brief time for prayer and song, followed by a relaxed social time over refreshments.

Each part of the evening begins with a short tour of the hosting church – not the entire building, only the worship area. Each youth group can decide how to lead the tour, but stress that there should be several people involved (and not just the clergy person!). The tour of the worship area should be brief, describing the significance of architecture, furniture, design, symbols, windows, art, banners, etc. Tour leaders should encourage questions from the group, but keep the group moving!

Our Christian Life Together

Graymoor (1995)

Presider: Our Christian life together is for the world and so reaches into our life together with the entire human community. Therefore, we pray for people of all living faiths and for those who do not believe.

Minister: For the unity of Christians,

Assembly: *that the churches of Rome, Constantinople, the churches of the East, and Canterbury, the churches of the Evangelical, Reformed and Free traditions may deepen their unity in Christ.*

M: For those in the office of oversight in our churches,

A: *that they may be living symbols of the unity of the church.*

M: For clergy and laity in the church,

A: *that all may live and minister to the gospel call to faith and faithfulness.*

M: For the newly baptized and for those preparing for baptism at Easter,

A: *that they may grow in faith, hope and charity.*

M: For Jewish people,

A: *that they may grow in faithfulness to their covenant with you.*

M: For Muslims,

A: *that they may deepen their faith-commitment to serve the will of God by creed, prayer, charity, fasting and pilgrimage.*

M: For those who believe in God under other names,

A: *that they may come more fully to your mystery.*

M: For those who do not believe in God,

A: *that they may long to find you and your peace.*

M: For all in public office and in human services,

A: *that they may work for justice, peace and the integrity of creation.*

M: For those in special need: travelers, the sick, the dying, the hungry, the oppressed, the homeless,

A: *that their sufferings may be relieved and that they may find fulfillment in you.*

M: For the needs of this gathered assembly,

A: open petitions

P: (*Prayer for Unity # 19 in* Celebrating Community)

Grant, O Lord, that your holy and life-giving Spirit may so move every human heart, that barriers which divide us may crumble, suspicions disappear and hatred cease; that, our divisions being healed, we may live in justice and peace, through Jesus Christ our Lord. Amen.

Blessing after a Meal

Canadian Council of Churches (1995)

Try a blessing and thanksgiving *after* a meal. Ahead of time, one person or several people are asked to be attentive to what about the mealtime itself might be brought to prayer after dinner is through. The whole group might wish to try to write a blessing together, or have a spontaneous thanksgiving time after the meal. The key is to keep the reflection particular and immediate. Here is an example from *Prayer of a Young Ghanaian Christian.*

> We thank you, Lord. That was such a good meal.
> The soup was good. The meat was good.
> The hot pepper and the yam were good.
> O Lord, our stomachs are full.
> Our bodies have what they need.
> This is a new miracle every day.
> We thank you for it and also for the good taste that lingers on our tongues.

How refreshing your water was!
With this meal you gave us strength required for the day.
Add to it your Spirit so that we might use your strength rightly.
Give us, besides food for our bodies,
your heavenly food for our whole life.
Praise be to you, merciful God. Amen.

Prayer of Thanksgiving

Canadian Council of Churches (1996)

Leader: Let us give thanks for the gifts and graces of each of the great expressions of Christ's Church:

For the *Roman Catholic Church*; its glorious traditions, its disciplines in holiness, its worship, rich with the religious passion of the centuries; its noble company of martyrs, doctors, and saints;

Congregation: *We thank you, Lord, and bless your holy name.*

L: For the *Protestant* and *Evangelical* communions; for their zealous proclamation of the gospel and their call to conversion;

C: *We thank you, Lord, and bless your holy name.*

L: For the *Anglican Church*, its way of mediation, and zeal for true and spiritual worship;

C: *We thank you, Lord, and bless your holy name.*

L: For the *Baptist* churches, emphasizing the primacy of personal regeneration and the conscious relation of the mature soul to one's Lord;

C: *We thank you, Lord, and bless your holy name.*

L: For the witness in the *United Church of Canada* to awaken the conscience of Christians to social evils, and for their emphasis on the witness of experience;

C: *We thank you, Lord, and bless your holy name.*

L: For the *Presbyterian* and *Reformed* reverence for the sovereignty of God and God's faithfulness to the covenant; for their sense of equality before God expressing itself in constitutional government;

C: *We thank you, Lord, and bless your holy name.*

L: For the *Orthodox* Churches; their treasures of mystical experience; their rich liturgy; their regard for the collective life and the common will as a source of authority;

C: *We thank you, Lord, and bless your holy name.*

L: For the witness to the inner light in every person borne by the *Religious Society of Friends* and their faithful ministry of non-violence and peacemaking;

C: *We thank you, Lord, and bless your holy name.*

L: For the *Pentecostal* movement, its enthusiasm, and its emphasis on the gifts of the spirit;

C: *We thank you, Lord, and bless your holy name.*

L: For the numerous *Free Churches*, who with humility and without ostentation, in slums and country place and town, speak the gospel to those unwelcomed or uninspired in other congregations;

C: *We thank you, Lord, and bless your holy name.*

L: For the *Uniting Churches* in all lands and for the struggle to overcome the divisions in the body of Christ, so that the world might believe;

C: *We thank you, Lord, and bless your holy name.*

All: *O God, grant to all these families within your great church,*
   that as they come from the east and from the west to sit down in your kingdom,
   each may lay at your feet that special gift and grace with which you have endowed it,
   in Christ. Amen.

(*adapted from a prayer written by the Right Reverend Terence Kelshaw for the 1995 conference of the U.S. National Association of Diocesan Ecumenical Officers*)

Welcome and Call to Worship

Graymoor (1997)

---

*Alleluia (*sung*)*

During the Alleluia a lighted candle is brought forward from the back of the church to the front. After three Alleluias, a pause is made in the procession and the presider says:

Presider: In the beginning was the Word: the Word was with God: the Word was God.

Assembly: *What has come into being in him was life, and the life was the light of all people.*

The Alleluia continues and a cross is brought forward. After three alleluias, a pause is made and the presider says:

P: God reconciled us to himself through Christ.

A: *And gave us the ministry of reconciliation.*

The Alleluia continues, and a Bible is brought forward.

P: Let the word of Christ dwell in you richly; teach and admonish one another in all wisdom.

A: *Sanctify us in the truth; your word is truth.*

The Alleluia continues until candle, cross and Bible are at the front. Then the presider says:

P: Let us pray.
Come, Jesus Christ, and open our ears to the longing of creation for renewal.
Come, Jesus Christ, and open our mouths to proclaim your kingdom.
Come, Jesus Christ, and open our eyes to the beauty of your creation.
Come, Jesus Christ, and open our hearts so that we may understand
that a new creation comes only through reconciliation in you.

A: *Amen.*

Prayer of Repentance

Canadian Council of Churches (1997)

Leader: Holy and Blessed Trinity,
Father, Son, and Holy Spirit,
one God in perfect communion,
look now on us, who look to you.

People: *We belong together.*

L: Members of one body, strands in one web, our communion is not whole.
United in faith and hope, our churches remain divided.

P: *We belong together.*

L: When one member suffers,
when one member rejoices,
the whole body gives thanks.

P: *We belong together.*

L: Forgive our disinterest,
our lack of compassion,
our acceptance of distance and division.

P: *We belong together.*
Kyrie eleison

Short silence

L: In Christ we are forgiven.

All: *Let us forgive others.*
In Christ we are restored:
let us restore others.
In Christ we are reconciled to God;
let us embrace the ministry of reconciliation.
Amen.

L: God of wonder,
you created every part of me,
knitting me in my mother's womb,
watching me grow according to your design:
so join together the children of your family
in one body, holy, vibrant, living,
dedicated to the glory of your name.

All: *Amen.*

Renewal of Ecumenical Commitment

Canadian Council of Churches (1998)

Representatives of different churches (Voices 1, 2 and 3) invite members of the congregation to renew their ecumenical commitment in these or similar words.

Voice 1: We have listened to the word of God and confessed our common faith,

Voice 2: We have prayed together, and shared the peace of Christ,

Voice 3: Now let us renew our commitment to find the unity Christ wills.

All: *The Spirit of God leads us towards a common path and raises hope within us.*
We believe that what unites us is stronger than that which divides us;
we want to listen to one another, attentive to the other's needs;
we want to bear one another's burdens, with respect and affection;
we want to recognize our differences as treasures and not as dangers;
we want to be renewed, so that we may be made one.
Trusting in God's Spirit, we commit ourselves
to work more closely for reconciliation, justice,
peace, and the preservation of creation.
Trusting in God's Spirit, we commit ourselves to prepare to receive the gift of unity.
Trusting in God's Spirit, we commit ourselves to overcome all obstacles
to our sharing of the eucharist at the table of the Lord.
The Spirit of God helps us in our weakness.
Nothing can separate us from the love of God.

Congregational Response of Faith

Canadian Council of Churches (1999)

Leader: Renewed in God's forgiveness, let us proclaim our faith in God:
Creator, Redeemer and Sustainer.

All: *We proclaim that God is with us in love, bringing all people together.*
Creator and life-giver, father and mother of us all regardless of race, gender or class:
you reveal yourself in justice, peace and love,
and desire for all peoples on earth your equity and truth.
We welcome Jesus Christ, our Saviour, God's beloved Son,
who was raised from the dead.
We commit our lives to Christ and his transforming power.
We reveal Christ's truth by challenging injustice and upholding faithfulness.
We resolve to live into being Christ's community of shalom.
We open our hearts to the coming of the Holy Spirit,
who breathes into us renewing power in the service of God's new community,
and leads us to live and work as one body for the good of all.
We joyfully believe that we are the church, called by God,
sent forth by Christ,
and led towards unity by the Holy Spirit, that the world may believe.
We are called to engage in the ministry of reconciliation,
that we may become a foretaste of God's new creation,
where all things are made new.

The Message of Revelation

Canadian Council of Churches (1999)

In the text chosen for this year's *Week of Prayer for Christian Unity* we see the culmination and fulfillment of the drama of salvation: God will dwell with humanity and recreate both heaven and earth. God's victory over the opposing powers, begun in the incarnation, is now accomplished. God, who delivered Israel from Egypt, is faithful and will deliver us from all oppressive and sinful powers. Revelation 21 expresses the Exodus tradition in a cosmic and final way: we are saved from the domination of human rulers but also from the demonic powers that are behind all sinful forces. Because God's rule cannot coexist with the destructive forces that rule the earth, God will renew all of creation, both heaven and earth, preparing a dwelling with us.

Exploring the Theme – John and his Dream

Today's story is about a particular dream. John, who had this dream, wrote the last book of our Bible, the book of Revelation. This John had been telling people about Jesus and was put in prison by the emperor for telling people that they should worship God, not the emperor. While John was a prisoner he wrote letters to his Christian friends. Close your eyes and imagine you are a group of his friends. One day you get this letter from John.

From the Island of Patmos

My dear, dear friends,

Do you remember how I wouldn't worship the Roman Emperor? I wouldn't give him gifts. And I wouldn't give him love or money, though some people treated him like God! But he is not God! I wanted to spread my good news about Jesus – about how Jesus lived and died for us many years ago; how he taught us to love and look after one another. This is God's way! The people in charge wanted Jesus to go away. When he died they tried to scare his followers away, too. They didn't want anyone to talk about Jesus. But look at how the story grew and how people kept on following him! You know, I never met Jesus, but I met others who shared Jesus' love with me.

And now, because I want to share that love too, I have been hurt. But don't worry, they didn't hit me or try to kill me. It's just that they've hurt me in the meanest way they possibly could – they took me away from you. It's as if they knew that they could hurt us the most by breaking our group apart. How can we build a new church without people? How can we pour out God's love from our church if we are broken?

But I must tell you about something that's just happened to me. I was sitting all by myself, and even though I was wide awake, I started to see all kinds of pictures in front of me – like a dream. It was so surprising. It's been so long since I've had a dream.

Then I really saw things! There were pictures in front of me and they were God's dreams: the earth was changing into something brand new; the holy city, Jerusalem, became shining and beautiful; heaven and earth seemed to reach out to kiss and hug each other; there was no more crying, no more pain. Everyone who was thirsty for God was getting a drink. Then I heard a voice telling me to write you about all of this. Even though I'm far, far away, I know you're with me, just as God is with us all. Tell everyone the good news of God's dream. Tell them it's our dream too.

May my words, my love, and my dreams reach out and touch you.

Your brother, John

Renewal of Commitment

Graymoor (1999)

"See, I am making all things new" (Revelation 21:5)

Leader: We are assembled here in gratitude to God,
turning always toward Christ, the conqueror of death:
We are God's people made strong in faith through baptism.

All: *We renew our commitment to live and witness for the unity of the body of Christ.*
We promise to work for communion in faith, life and witness,
so that, as one body, by the one Spirit,
we may be witnesses to the perfect unity of God's love.
We renew our commitment to engage in mission in faithfulness to Christ,
to take up the cross,
to proclaim the gospel,
to love and serve others,
to resist evil and struggle for peace and justice,
to use earth's resources with care,
and to risk all for the sake of Christ's kingdom.
We renew our commitment to ecumenism so that,
through united witness and service,
the churches may again be effective voices and instruments
for the fulfillment of God's will in our age.

L: As a sign of our renewed commitment to baptism and its consequences, I invite you to come forward, to dip your hand in this water, and to receive it in blessing, for the scripture says: "I will give water as a gift from the spring of the water of life" (Revelation 21:6).

A hymn, song or anthem may be sung as the assembly receives the water in blessing.

2000 and onwards ...

The dawning of the third millennium brought with it a number of serious issues and events: from techno-anxiety to the environment; from September 11, 2001, to war in Iraq and Afghanistan; from immigration to the death of Pope John Paul II. The celebration and fragile ambiguity of the turn of this millennium set the tone for Week of Prayer for Christian Unity themes. Marking this moment meant myriad things to people around the world; not surprisingly, Christians differed in their chosen approaches to celebrations.

In the midst of fireworks and countdowns, wars and poverty continued and many made big money off millennial anxieties. While a Jubilee was declared by the Pope and significant strides were made in Third World debt relief, these were met by an even stronger sense of failure regarding what had still not been achieved. Millennial goals for fighting child poverty in Canada remained unmet. The cross is ever with us, but with the cross comes the promise of resurrection. Celebration and fragility were gathered up within the theme of the Week of Prayer for the year 2000. *Gathered in Christ* set an appropriately christocentric focus not just for that year but for the whole decade. Jesus is central throughout the decade, as the one who heals and opens lips, who is the fountain of life, the living waters, whose name gathers us all. The strength of focus on the incarnation of God in Jesus Christ means that one is never far away from the cross, the fragility of human life, and the brokenness of the body of Christ.

Confronted by the realities of the incarnation, the cross and the resurrection, Christians are called to conversion, to return to the fountain of life, to be gathered up with one another in Christ, to turn to the wounded header, to *allow* oneself to be healed. From 2002:

> The symbol of the fountain invites us to seek the source of the life we share. It recalls our need to return to the origin, to the principle, the roots, the essential. To walk together, Christians need to be grounded in the Word of God, the revelation of God's face in Jesus Christ, the renewing power of God's Spirit, the discovery of the love of God, Father, Son and Holy Spirit. Without light from the source of all light, the problems we encounter remain shrouded in darkness and become insurmountable. The fountain is an image for water welling up abundantly. It suggests the springs of water that gush forth as a source of life in dry lands. The Bible highlights the symbolic and theological richness of water's life-giving and cleansing qualities. Faith, prayer and common action can make water spring even from the desert rock of bitterness. The water that flows from the side of the crucified Lord (John 19:34) can cleanse the sin of Christian division.

To pray for unity is to enter into the depths of the wounded Christ's body, to touch the wounds of our brothers and sisters in Christ, and our own wounds – to see in all human fragility and brokenness the presence of the broken Christ. This prayer is itself an act of fragility, of the sort that St. Paul described when he wrote of experiencing strength in weakness. It is not that strength comes out of weakness, in a linear sort of way, though it can and does do so in terms of human experience. Rather, as this decade's Week of Prayer materials express, it is within the act and experience of entering into the woundedness of the world and of the Church that the cross is met with the promise of resurrection and true communion is glimpsed.

J.E. Scully

Gathered in Christ

Canadian Council of Churches (2000)

Doxology

Leader 1: Blessed be God, Father of our Lord Jesus Christ,

Congregation: *who has blessed us in Christ with every spiritual blessing.*

L2: Holy and blessed Trinity, one God, glory to you!
 O Source of all being, Creator of the world,
 you have spoken to us your word, declaring your love,
 and so have given us the gift of yourself for all time.

C: *Amen. We adore you.*

L3: Holy and blessed Trinity, one God, glory to you!
 Eternal Wisdom, incarnate Word of God,
 out of your love for us,
 you have chosen to share our life
 and to live our death.

C: *Amen. We adore you.*

L4: Holy and blessed Trinity, one God, glory to you!
 O Holy Spirit, unbounded power of love,
 you continually draw us into new life and hope,
 in communion with God and all creation.

L1: Praise, glory, and thanksgiving be given to the Father,
 the Son, and the Holy Spirit, now and forever, in all places and at all times.

C: *Amen.*

L1: Let us pray:
 O God,
 you have gathered us together from different churches
 that we might listen to you, pray to you,
 and praise you with united hearts and voices.
 We ask you to strengthen our desire for unity
 so that the world may see and believe;
 through Jesus, the Saviour of all.

C: *Amen.*

Sending Forth

L1: In Christ, we have come to know
    that God's heart is open to us.
    Therefore, let us open our hearts to one another.
    The peace of Christ be with you.

C: *Peace be with you.*

A sign of peace may be exchanged.

Distribution of the Light

L1: Jesus says: "I am the Light of the world."
    Jesus says also: "You are the light of the world.
    Let your light shine before others that they may see your good works,
    and give glory to your Father in heaven."

L5: May the light of the new creation, which appeared in Christ,
    inflame us, and spread its rays through us into the world.
    We have been enriched with the fullness of God's blessing,
    and we have been given the task of carrying the light of Christ into the world.

Lighting a candle from the large candle on or near the table, the worship leaders share that light with those nearby, saying, "The light of Christ"; the light is then passed on from candle to candle. When all candles have been lit, the congregation stands.

Blessing

L1: God, who gave us the light of eternal life and love,
    enlightens us on our way,
    inflames us with courage and hope,
    inspires our thinking and our doing.

L5: God has given us a common vocation.
    Go in peace to love and serve together in Christ's name.

C. *May the grace of our Lord Jesus Christ, the love of God,
    and the communion of the Holy Spirit be with us all.
    Amen.*

Your Cross Points the Way

Graymoor (2001)

Leader: Let us look to Jesus, the pioneer and perfecter of our faith.
Jesus Christ, we look upon your cross.
We come to you and stand before your cross.

All: *Your cross is showing us the way.*

L: Your cross points the way from separation to unity,

All: *because you sacrificed yourself for all of us.*

L: Your cross points the way from death to life,

A: *because you defeated death for ever.*

L: Your cross points the way from sadness to joy.

A. *Your resurrection calls us to rejoice in a joy that nobody can take from us.*

L: Jesus Christ, you are the resurrection and the life. We worship you.

All: *Glory to the Father and to the Son and to the Holy Spirit. Amen.*

The Fountain of Life

Canadian Council of Churches (2002)

Leader: Your steadfast love, O God, reaches to the heavens.

Response: *For with you is the fountain of life; in your light we see light.*

L: We come before you, longing to form a human community of reconciliation
between young and old, men and women, crossing our various cultures.
We seek to overcome the disunity of the Christian Church.
We place ourselves and our world in the shadow of your wings.

R: *For with you is the fountain of life; in your light we see light.*

L: When we lose courage in the journey toward wholeness,
when the unity we seek seems an elusive dream,
when our divisions make the way of our journey dark,
help us to turn to your love and see your hopeful dream.

R: *For with you is the fountain of life; in your light we see light.*

L: When we are the very barriers we have built
through our own suspicions and lack of trust,
send us the strength to remove walls
that divide us from our brothers and sisters,
and courage to listen to the fears and concerns others have about us.
Help us to reach out to each other in love.

R: *For with you is the fountain of life; in your light we see light.*

L: We pray for the churches and the Christians of the world
who are committed to a way of deeper co-operation.
Awaken in all of us a spirit of discernment, harmony and confidence,
and make of us a full community of love
gathered at your great feast of grace.

R: *For with you is the fountain of life; in your light we see light.*

L: We pray for the people of our world
so often torn by war or suffering from disaster.
We pray also for all in our own country
who experience abuse at the hands of others,
who are homeless or in deep poverty,
who despair of any change in their lives.
We also pray for all who would bring light
into the darkened corners of our world.
May they be your healing messengers to the world.
May we also be challenged to such ministry,
where we live, as followers of Christ.

R: *For with you is the fountain of life; in your light we see light.*

Prayer of Repentance

Graymoor (2002)

This prayer is inspired by the prayer of repentance used at the Second European Ecumenical Assembly, Graz, Austria 1997. A period of silence prepares our recognition of our faults and our asking for forgiveness.

Leader: Eternal and almighty God, you do not spurn that which you have created,
and you forget the faults of those who repent.
Create and awaken in us a new and contrite heart
so that we may be sorry for our sins, recognize our wickedness

and receive from you, God of mercy, pardon and peace, through Jesus Christ our Lord.

All: *Amen.*

L: Let us ask for the forgiveness of God and of each other
for the divisions that have hindered Christian witness.
Lord, we have sinned against you and against our neighbors.

All: *Lord, have mercy.*

L: O Christ, our divisions are contrary to your will
and weaken our common witness to you.

All: *Christ, have mercy.*

L: Lord, we have not loved you enough in our brothers and sisters created in your image
but different from us.

All: *Lord, have mercy.*

L: God, you have created us; let us no longer live next to each other as strangers.
Satisfy the longings of our hearts and grant our petitions.
Unite us soon in one holy church through your Son Jesus Christ
who lives and reigns with you in the communion of the Holy Spirit forever and ever.
Amen.

Come, Holy Spirit

Canadian Council of Churches (2003)

Each reader may move to stand beside the clay jar and/or the central candle as the prayer progresses. The congregation may say or sing a petition to the Holy Spirit at appropriate points.

Reader 1: We bring to mind, O God, the frailty of our Christian witness,
and of our ecumenical achievement.
Let us pray for renewal, in the power of the Holy Spirit,
of our gifts in sharing the light of Christ,
and the strength of our common love of Christ.

Congregation: *Come, Holy Spirit; breathe your light into our souls.*

R2: We bring to mind, O God, the suffering, evil and despair in your world,
and our failure to address them in consistent and just ways.
Let us pray for eyes to see, ears to hear,

and hearts to understand the possibilities for a restored world,
and for strength to witness faithfully to the love of God.

C: *Come, Holy Spirit; breathe your light into our hearts.*

R3: We bring to mind, O God,
the many demands placed on those who carry your mission of love and mercy
to a world that hungers for peace and justice.
Let us pray for endurance, perseverance and confidence
in spreading the Good News of Christ.

C: *Come, Holy Spirit; breathe your light into our lives.*

R4: In Thanksgiving, we praise you, O Holy One,
for your embrace of the treasures we bring in our earthen vessels,
and for your gift of the light of the world, Jesus our Redeemer.

C: *Amen.*

In the Image of Christ
Canadian Council of Churches (2003)

God of love, powerful creator of all life, encourage us to discern in ourselves and in each of our brothers and sisters your image and resemblance. Give us the strength necessary to obey the imperative of your all-embracing love. God of love, we pray that our witness will lead to the unity of the churches, and that with one voice we may call upon all humanity to be responsible for creation and for our neighbour. Through Jesus Christ, our Lord, we pray. Amen.

"My Peace I Give You"
Canadian Council of Churches (2004)

Homiletical Helps

Christ's offer of peace goes far beyond the kind of peace that the world gives, and yet, Christ reveals to us the peace that is in the world. Although it is filled with turmoil, poverty, violence and war, the world has the Dominion of God buried in it like a treasure buried in a field, like a seed germinating in the earth. Over and over again, "amid the world's bleak wilderness," Christ offers us glimpses of God's reign of justice, mercy and peace. Amid the divisions of the church, God's reign is poised, ready to be ushered into a world desperate for Christ's promise of peace. Amid the brokenness of our lives, Christ provides the treasures we need to bring about God's reign.

A proclamation that works as leaven in the dough will both present glimpses of the reign of God in the world and point to the work of the Spirit who inspires the Body of Christ in the work of ushering in the reign of God. Empowered and accompanied by the Holy Spirit, the community of believers that is the church is bound together by love: love for God, love for one another, love for neighbours, love for strangers and love for enemies.

Prayer of Praise
(from the Syriac Liturgy)

Leader: In your light we shall see light, Jesus full of light;
   you are the true light which illumines the whole creation;
   enlighten us with your joyous light, splendour of the Father in heaven.
   Pure and holy one who dwells in the habitations of light,
   keep us from evil passions and thoughts of hatred
   and grant that we may do deeds of justice with purity of heart.
   On this holy day, which has brought us together,
   we implore you to grant unity to your church:
   keep us in the fullness of your peace.

All: *Amen.*

L: Let us thank God the Father, Lord of all;
 let us adore his only Son and glorify his Holy Spirit
 in giving our life into his keeping and begging for his mercy.

All: *Have pity on us, O God, merciful and good.*

Intercessions
(from the Syriac Liturgy)

Voice 1: Let us make our petitions to God Almighty,
   Father of our God and Saviour Jesus Christ:
   We pray you Lord, in your graciousness,
   Friend of all, remember your one, holy, universal and apostolic church.

V2: *(Prayers for the local church community are offered)*

All: *We pray for the peace of the one, holy, universal and apostolic church.*

V1: Bless these creatures spread from one end of the world to the other,
 all peoples and herds.
 May your peace come down from the heavens into all hearts,

peace to this generation, and fulfill us with your grace.
O King of Peace, clothe all with peace:
the governments, armies, leaders of nations, our neighbours,
immigrants, refugees and expatriates.
Give us your Peace, for from you come all things.
May we belong to you, O God our Lord, for we know only you.
We proclaim your Holy Name.
May our souls live in your Holy Spirit.
May the deathly power of sin not prevail upon your servants,
nor upon any people of the earth.

V2: *(Prayers for local concerns and peace are offered)*

All: *Kyrie Eleison or Lord, have mercy.*

V1: Let us pray to God Almighty,
Father of our Lord and Saviour Jesus Christ.
We beg your graciousness, O Friend of all.
Remember our gatherings in the name of your holy church,
bless them and let them spread throughout all the earth.

Voice 2: *(Prayers for the unity of the local church are offered)*

All: *We pray for this church.*

V1: You have reconciled the creatures of the earth with those of heaven
and you have made them one.
You have accomplished your plan in the flesh
and as your body rose into heaven,
you filled the universe with your holiness.
You said to your disciples and to the holy apostles:
"I leave you peace, I give you my peace."
Now, Lord of peace, grant us these blessings;
purify us from all sin, from all duplicity, from all hypocrisy, from all evil,
from all machinations and the memory of evil hidden by death.
Clothe us with perpetual peace
so that we may keep the trust of the apostolic faith
and may live united by the ties of charity.

All: *Kyrie Eleison* or *Lord, have mercy.*

V2: Decree for us your peace, that we may all become,
in the unity of the faith, a perfect being measuring up to the fullness of Christ.

All: *Kyrie Eleison* or *Lord, have mercy.*

V1: Bless, O Lord, the peace of your church,
all your people and all your creatures.
Reconcile all enemies and belligerents,
that their swords may be transformed into plowshares,
and their spears into pruning hooks, that they may learn war no more.
And keep them all in your name.

All: *Kyrie Eleison* or *Lord, have mercy.*

V2: Lord, save your people and bless your inheritance;
watch over and keep it for ever.
Maintain it in the true faith in glory and dignity all the days:
establish it in the love and peace which surpasses all things.

All: *Kyrie Eleison* or *Lord, have mercy.*

V1: O Holy Spirit, make us worthy of contributing
to the sanctification of your heavenly treasures
and of offering a true adoration in purity and holiness here and in all places,
now and all the days of our lives,
that your good news may be proclaimed unto the ends of the earth.

All: *Kyrie Eleison* or *Lord, have mercy.*

We Praise You, Lord

Canadian Council of Churches (2005)

Leader 1: Thus speaks the Lord Jesus:
Because I love you, O my people, I was born in Bethlehem.
They named me Emmanuel, for I am God with you, for ever and ever.

Congregation: *We praise you, Lord.*

L2: I was baptized in the water of the Jordan
and the Father called me the Beloved, as a sign of the baptism in the Spirit.

C: *We praise you, Lord.*

L1: I was led by the Spirit into the desert to confront the Tempter,
to take on the human struggle against sin and evil.

C: *We praise you, Lord.*

L2: I proclaimed the good news of the reign of the Father,
a reign of justice and mercy, love and truth, peace and joy.

I accomplished the signs of the new era –
my hands cured the sick, my presence brought peace.

C: *We praise you, Lord.*

L2: I broke bread and offered new wine to renew God's covenant with you
and to give you life in all its fullness.
I prayed to the Father that my joy might be in you.

C: *We praise you, Lord.*

L2: I died on a cross of wood,
for the forgiveness of sins and to bring back the scattered children,
and I opened the gates of hell. On the third day God raised me from the dead.

C: *We praise you, Lord.*

L1: From my place beside the Father, I breathe upon you the Holy Spirit,
who will remind you of all that I have taught you,
who is the breath of life, who is light and consolation,
the force of your witness and the inspiration of your prayer.

C: *We praise you, Lord.*

L2: Listen to me, O my people, for I am with you every day
until the end of time, that you may be *one* with me as I am *one* with my Father,
that the world might believe.
Listen to my voice, my people,
and follow me so that there is but one flock and one Shepherd.

C: *We praise you, Lord.*

Response of praise (said or sung)

L: Blessed be God and Father of our Lord Jesus Christ,
who has blessed us in Christ with every spiritual blessing! *(Ephesians 1)*

Prayer for forgiveness

Loving God, you have given us Jesus Christ, our foundation.
We confess that we have not always built well upon that foundation.
Have mercy on us.
Forgive us and grant us a fresh chance to work together for the unity of your church.
Amen.

Confession and Pardon

Graymoor (2005)

Between each expression of repentance, members of the congregation come forward, taking a stone from the container and placing the stone at the foot of the plain cross that has been brought in at the procession, as a symbol of Christ as foundation of the church. This gesture expresses our desire for conversion and our renewed belonging in Christ for the construction of the one church.

Leader 1: Lord, you are peace and reconciliation!

Leader 2: Forgive us, Lord, for often choosing jealousy and animosity rather than confidence and respect between the churches.

Silence and the placing of stones at the foot of the cross.

L1: Lord, you give us an abundance of blessings in the unity of faith!

L2: Forgive us, Lord, for often choosing isolation and refusing to be a blessing for each other, between churches.

Silence and the placing of stones at the foot of the cross.

L1: Lord, you have given joy to the afflicted, freedom to captives, pardon to sinners!

L2: Forgive us, Lord, for having closed our hands and turned our faces away from those who need help.

Silence and the placing of stones at the foot of the cross.

L1: Lord, you have gathered us together as a shepherd gathers his flock and then goes to seek the one sheep that is lost!

L2: Forgive us, Lord, for having often strayed far from you, pushing each other away and underlining our divisions.

Silence and the placing of stones at the foot of the cross.

Gathered in My Name

Canadian Council of Churches (2006)

Sending Forth

L: As we go forth from this place,
    we pray to God to bless our journey together:

All: *Open our eyes to your presence.*
    Open our ears to your call.
    Open our hearts to your love.
    May we open our arms to others.
    May we open our hearts to strangers.
    May we open our doors to callers.
    That we may be open to you, Lord
    Open this day for evermore.★

L: May the grace of the Lord Jesus Christ, the love of God
    and the fellowship of the Holy Spirit be with us all, now and forever.

All: *Amen.*

(*★words: Irish song [8th century], tr. Mary E. Byrne, 1905; versed by Eleanor H. Hull, 1912*)

The Presence of Christ

Graymoor (2006)

Leader: Jesus, Risen Lord –

All: *We gather in your name.*

L: Jesus, Good Shepherd –

All: *We gather in your name.*

L: Jesus, Word of life –

All: *We gather in your name.*

L: Jesus, friend of the poor –

All: *We gather in your name.*

L: Jesus, source of all forgiveness –

All: *We gather in your name.*

L: Jesus, Prince of Peace –

All: *We gather in your name.*

All: *Lord Jesus Christ, you call us together in faith and love*
Breathe again the new life of your Holy Spirit upon us,
that we may hear your holy word,
pray in your name,
seek unity among Christians,
and live more fully the faith we profess.
All glory and honour be yours,
with the Father, and the Holy Spirit, forever and ever. Amen.

"Doing Everything Well" (Mark 7:31-37)

Rick Fee, General Secretary of the Life and Mission Agency
and past Moderator of The Presbyterian Church in Canada
Canadian Council of Churches (2007)

The world has been bringing people to Jesus since his days on earth, when they brought people such as the deaf man who had a speech impediment. We model our response after Jesus. We have read, we have preached, we have proclaimed that our Jesus "did everything well." Like the crowds of followers around Jesus on that miracle day, we have zealously proclaimed this miracle and urged all others to come to Jesus and be likewise healed

Sadly, the track record of Jesus' followers has not been so laudable, as we can see in "the worst humanitarian disaster we have ever faced," as Stephen Lewis, UN Special Envoy for AIDS in Africa, has called AIDS.

When AIDS was brought to the churches, they did not do everything well. It was easier for churches to put forth the God of judgment and condemnation. God was a reprimanding and chastizing power. God was sending punishment. God was weeding and winnowing.

The Church in the 1980s and early 1990s largely hid the Father welcoming home the prodigal son (Luke 15:11-32). Those diagnosed with this illness were left to walk the road to Emmaus by themselves (Luke 24:13-35). There was no God as Immanuel – God-with-us. There was no healing. The message of Jesus was blocked. There was no healing of tongue and ear so that a message of compassion could be proclaimed and heard. Besides their death sentences, those suffering untold pain and agony had to endure further isolation, ostracism and turmoil. Not much was done well.

The Church hid behind the claim of being the resurrected body of Jesus Christ. There was certainly no thought that this body would ever declare that it had AIDS. There were no messages of forgiveness, love or welcome. There was, however, much condemnation. The Church was deaf. The Church was mute. The Church stood in need of healing. In such a state, the Church contributed to the silence, perpetuated the shame, compounded the humiliation, and ensured that the stigma fell upon anyone who received a doctor's verdict.

Colin Powell, a five-star general, described the tiny little virus called HIV as the greatest weapon of mass destruction of them all. U2 rock star Bono declared that it was the Church's response to AIDS that almost made his cynicism about religion and Christianity return, saying: "The religious community, in large part, missed it. The people who didn't miss it could only see it as divine retribution for bad behaviour – even on children – even on the fastest-growing group of HIV infections who were married, faithful women." However, at the 2006 Washington Prayer Breakfast, Bono admitted that he had revised his opinion of the Church, noting, "The Church was slow, but the Church eventually got busy on this 'leprosy of our age'."

Stephen Lewis says churches are becoming vital participants in the war against the pandemic. "The role of the religious leaders is increasingly crucial," Lewis points out. "It started very slowly. But in the last three or four years religious leadership moved a long way."

Indeed, the Church has made a journey. The Church has once again been brought to its Master. We have seen – or perhaps have even discovered for the first time – that each human being is created in the image of God. God as a forgiving father has been brought to bear. The God of the possibility of new life has emerged. The God of resurrection power has emerged. The God waiting to welcome us just as we are has touched us.

As this disease is brought to Jesus in our generation by those who beg to have hands laid on them, the Church has moved from a negative image of God. Today the Church proclaims the power of a resurrected God who overcomes death, destruction, disease and despair. Our God speaks of peace and welcome. We proclaim that no one is worthy, perfect, acceptable, and that we all come as we are – not to a moody, angry and judging God, but to a forgiving God, a healing God.

The Church has learned that neither people living with HIV and AIDS nor God is to be blamed for the disease. The Church has learned that God's love and works may be revealed through those living with this disease.

In our dealing with this disease we have been reintroduced to the God of the stable and of the cross, the God who does not condemn the world but who does everything well, especially unstopping the ears and loosening the tongues so that those people who have seen and believed may zealously proclaim the goodness of God.

May Our Ears Be Opened

Graymoor (2007)

From the start of a hymn or chant, sung in the manner of Taizé or Iona, or perhaps the charismatic chorus "Open my eyes, Lord, I want to see Jesus," a large cross is carried in by four young persons and laid on the floor. They stand around it, praying silently. The singing will give way to the following introduction to the moment of silence. It would also be possible to lead the congregation into the moment's silence with a few bars of music.

Introduction to the moment of silence

L: Let us keep silence before God … silent within ourselves … opening our hearts to the silence of our sisters and brothers living in suffering: "if one member suffers, all suffer together" (1 Cor 12:26). May our ears be opened by this silence in communion with those whose voices we do not hear, either because they keep silent or they are silenced. Let us hear the call of Christ rather than remain deaf. He teaches that we should allow ourselves, like him, to feel the suffering of others. In this, we are united as one church.

Three minutes of silence

Song / Chant / Hymn

The hymn of introduction to the moment of silence is taken up again by a soloist, singing gradually louder. Then the whole congregation joins in.

Prayer

Leader: O God who reigns in heavenly splendor, you have broken the silence through the revelation of your Word, Jesus Christ, who came forth from the heart of your silence and was hidden from the Prince of this world.

All: *Open our eyes that we may see Jesus,*
the star who dispels our shadows.
Open our ears that we might hear the voices muffled in the silence of millions,
those voices muffled by the trials and suffering of this transient world.
Open our hearts that we may know how to respond to the pain
of those who suffer among us,
as the woman of Bethany pouring perfume on Jesus' head,
and like Simon of Cyrene who without complaint carried your Son's cross,
reduced to silence by those who attacked him.

L: Assembled here together, we shatter the silence with the words of the prayer that Jesus taught us.

All: *Our Father …*

As a sign of God's blessing, of the consolation of his word and his presence, as the congregation disperses, each person might receive a drop of perfume into his or her hands to pass this to others – a tradition in Orthodox churches.

A Life-Giving Work

Canadian Council of Churches (2007)

Above all, relax and enjoy the experience! Let the occasion show you the gifts God has in store for you. Much has already been achieved in ecumenism, with the help of the *Week of Prayer for Christian Unity*, which has been celebrated regularly since 1908. The time and energy you take to prepare and celebrate the Ecumenical Worship Service, and any other activities you take on together, will be part of the fulfillment of Christ's prayer "that they may be one" (John 17:22). Let us pray for one another, and rejoice in one another, as we prepare ourselves for this celebration.

> An ineffable change takes place by which our prayer is stripped, to be re-clothed in Jesus' prayer…. This manner of prayer does not, of course, erase, weaken or obscure in any way the differences of doctrine which characterize our separations. Each one is fully conscious of this and recognizes it: thus each remains true to self and sincere toward others. But this kind of prayer, with a great sweep of wings, rises above all differences, and makes it possible for us all to rest together in the heart of Christ.
>
> —*Abbé Paul Couturier, Founder of the "Octave of Prayer for Christian Unity"*

Prayer

God our Creator, we gaze at the splendour of the creation by your Word. When our lives fall into ruin, we beg you to renew your marvellous works. Despite the scandal of our divisions, we can pray with one voice: that your Word never cease to make all things new in the heart of our broken lives. Give us courage to be artisans of creation and of unity as you are. Amen.

Pray without Ceasing

Canadian Council of Churches (2008)

The apostle Paul writes, *"Rejoice always, pray without ceasing, give thanks in all circumstances; for this is the will of God in Christ Jesus for you."* His epistle is written to a faithful community that is anxious about death. Many good and believing brothers and sisters have *fallen asleep* before the Lord's return to bring all into his resurrection. What will happen to these faithful dead? What will happen to the living? Paul assures them that the dead shall be raised with the living and exhorts them to *pray without ceasing.* But what does it mean to *pray without ceasing?*

When the people of God found themselves in exile – when all seemed hopeless and dry – the words upon the prophet Isaiah's lips were *"Seek the Lord while he may be found, call upon him while he is near"* (Isaiah 55:6). Even in exile, the Lord was near, urging the people to pray, that they might know God's mercy and pardon. Likewise, Psalm 34 affirms the prophetic conviction that God will answer those who call upon the Lord, and adds praise to the call to *pray without ceasing.*

As Christians in search of unity, our call to *"pray without ceasing"* becomes our eternal intercession to the Father: *"that all may be one, …that the world may believe …"* (John 17:21).

Epilogue

Working on this anthology has been a blessing. When the three of us agreed to form the editing team we had no idea what would be ahead of us. Two of us worked on this while moving from one parish to another. Yet, while we worked on it there were many times of laughter and joy. A few observations stand out for all of us. It seems odd to us that no other organization or group is undertaking the work of putting together such an anthology. Looking back, hearing, learning, and remembering the prayers of the faithful through the ages keeps us humble. Going over all this material reminds us how many have prayed, have invested time and energy and credibility among their peers all the while holding out the vision of Christ – as we draw closer in unity to Christ we draw closer to one another and the world catches a glimpse of the glory and beauty of Christ.

Various archives and denominations have kept some records of these yearly documents, but no one organization has them complete. Perhaps that is an important lesson on record-keeping for the churches. Looking back is every bit as important as looking ahead.

Another observation is what a blessing it has been for us to work with Christians from the various traditions. We each have different emphases and strengths and as we shared these we grew in our appreciation for the presence and the work of the Spirit in drawing us together in Christ. As we talked about this we realized that the material for the Week of Prayer has been written by a variety of people from many different denominations. It would be so interesting to know the denominations of the various writers of prayers and litanies as this sometimes gives a depth of insight and context to what is written in particular times and decades.

As this material was gathered and we read it we realized our words and works and efforts are added to prayers and sighs and hopes and tears of sisters and brothers in Christ who have faithfully served before. As the editing team sat in St. Cuthbert's we had a quiet glimpse of the dedication and visionary purpose of the men and women who worked on these liturgies and prayers. In the height of the Second World War a few faithful people prepared materials to guide the prayers of Christians around the world. In the context of violence and death and war some of the faithful challenged and invited others to join in prayers for unity. We are reminded that the focus is not on denominations or on institutions; our focus was and remains on Christ. He taught us to pray. Over the years men and women quietly, regularly and faithfully followed Christ and prayed His prayer for unity. May all who come behind us find us just as faithful.

Respectfully submitted in His service:

Richard T. Vander Vaart
Judee Archer Green
Mary Marrocco
October 2007

Acknowledgments

Rick Fee, General Secretary, Life and Mission Agency, The Presbyterian Church in Canada

One of the great challenges we had at the start of this project was gathering the necessary material for the anthology. One hundred years of material was liberally scattered in various interesting likely and unlikely places. The World Council of Churches did have some material in its library in Geneva; unfortunately, our budget did not allow us to go there and search for it. Rick rode to our rescue. He was travelling to Geneva on business for the Presbyterian Church in Canada and graciously consented to pick it up for us.

Gisèle Bourrel, Librarian, World Council of Churches, Geneva

Though we live in an age of convenient communication, including faxes, telephones and the ubiquitous e-mail, there still needs to be a live person who responds to requests. Gisèle graciously answered the call to gather material on the Week of Prayer for Christian Unity – any and all material available from the World Council of Churches library. Where duplicate copies were available, she gave us originals; otherwise, she had photocopies made of rare or scarce resources.

Gail Allan, Program Coordinator, Interfaith Education and Relations, United Church of Canada

"It is not what you know but who you know." That familiar cliché is regularly confirmed by experience. As the idea for this anthology was developed, the initial difficulty was finding and gathering material. Gail connected our information-gathering team with Gisèle Bourrel, the World Council of Churches librarian in Geneva. Gail was a key link in the information chain.

Bernice Baranowski, Coordinator of the Ecumenical Library at the Canadian Centre for Ecumenism in Montreal

It is altogether too tempting to search farther from home rather than consider resources and materials in our own backyard. Bernice is the librarian at the Canadian Centre for Ecumenism in Montreal – a great resource right here in Canada. We are grateful that she found much of the material we have for this anthology. On very short notice she went to great lengths to find material and make copies.

Paul Ladouceur, Orthodox Church in America, and Moira Barclay-Fernie, Presbyterian Church in Canada

Paul and Moira made the trip to downtown Montreal on their own time to find, gather and photocopy the material for this anthology – a wonderful help.

Veronica Sullivan, Graymoor Friars

All the enthusiasm and all the plans the editing team had for this project hung on a single peg – finding material. After several weeks of fruitless searching and nearly giving up on the project there was one final chance to find material – the archives at Graymoor. Veronica went to work, found the pieces we needed and gave us fresh enthusiasm and hope that enough material could be gathered to make this project worthwhile.

J. Eileen Scully, Anglican Church of Canada

Eileen was an enthusiastic participant on the Canadian Council of Churches' Week of Prayer for Christian Unity Writing Team for many years. The original idea for this anthology was hers, and she mentioned it to several people. God has certainly answered the prayers of the people fervently prayed in country gatherings and grand cathedrals; God has given glimpses and signs of the unity that is ours in Christ. God has used the materials produced to guide our prayers for unity and it made sense to follow up on Eileen's idea with this anthology. As Eileen's term on the Writing Team was completed, a few members of the team carried her idea forward. A few simple inquiries revealed that the World Council of Churches and the Graymoor Friars did not have plans for an anthology commemorating these hundred years. This realization stoked our passion for this project all the more. As events unfolded, Eileen became one of the project's editors, as well, doing the historical research and preparing the summary of the first 40 years as well as the introductions to the next six decades. Her contributions have been invaluable.

Fred Graham, United Church of Canada

As an editing team, Judee, Mary and Richard were immediately concerned with what to do with the growing stack of materials we had gathered. We realized we'd need a skilled editor to pull the material together. Fred Graham's name regularly came up as someone with a passion for prayer and for ecumenism who had the right skills to edit the material.

Fred was very willing and enthused; however, there was one proviso. He had been on the waiting list for a liver transplant for almost a year. Should a liver become available, we'd have to find another editor. Within weeks, Fred got the news: a suitable liver was found! The surgery went well, and we give thanks to God for God's care to Fred and his family during this time.

May God grant continued grace and healing to Fred Graham and success to this project that is so close to his heart.

Bernadette Gasslein

Bernadette, an accomplished liturgist and editor, was able to step in as text editor and meet the tight deadlines required by the publisher so the anthology could be available for the 100th anniversary. She scoured a huge amount of material, selecting liturgies and prayers that stand out as excellent on their own or clearly spoke to a particular era.

Ferdinanda Van Gennip

Certain texts were available only in French. Ferdinanda Van Gennip provided wonderful translations in record time, and with a sincere enthusiasm for the content.

Karen Teasdale, United Church of Canada

Karen has been volunteering at the Canadian Council of Churches for over a year. As materials poured in from Geneva, Montreal and New York, Karen made five copies of everything for our editing team and the two editors. She completed this fussy, time-consuming work quickly, efficiently and with a good spirit, and has continued to work to ensure that this collected body of archives will be available in future.

Mary Delph, Administrative Assistant, Canadian Council of Churches

Early on in this project, it was hoped that much of the material could simply be scanned to create electronic documents; unfortunately, the poor printing quality of the original material made this impractical and all of it needed to be retyped. Mary spent many evenings and weekends faithfully and carefully typing the texts you will read here.

Nancy Hurn, Archivist, Anglican Church of Canada, and Mary-Anne Nicholls, Archivist, Diocese of Toronto, Anglican Church of Canada

The material prepared for the Week of Prayer for Christian Unity was sometimes a single sheet of paper; other times it was a booklet filled with resources. (During World War II, the material was produced in England and it was a single sheet.) Many thanks to Nancy and Mary-Anne for searching out material for this project – it was often difficult to describe what exactly the material might look like. Furthermore, it is good to note that various denominations have been keeping some records of this week of prayer. Linda Nicholls (Anglican Church of Canada) gave us the names of these two contact people.

Kevin Burns, Editorial Director, English Publications, Novalis

This project caught Kevin Burns's attention right away, and his enthusiasm was contagious. He was instrumental in helping our editing team flesh out what needed to be done, organizing a reasonable timeline for the project, and helping us sort out copyright issues.

Anne Louise Mahoney, Managing Editor, Novalis

Anne Louise Mahoney has been a steady, patient, faithful counsellor and adviser to our editing team right from the start. No question was too foolish or too small for her consideration. Her help was greatly appreciated. It is a delight to work with Anne Louise each year on the Canadian edition of the Week of Prayer for Christian Unity kit.

Forest City Community Church, Dresden, and St. Cuthbert's Presbyterian Church, Hamilton

The editing team members live in Toronto, Hamilton and Dresden. As much as possible, the work was carried out via phone and e-mail. Once in a while, though, we had to have face-to-face meetings. One of our earliest meetings was in a café in London. This proved to be cramped quarters; we needed a place where we could spread out materials and examine and group them according to decade or interest or usability. Pastor Rob Hogendoorn and the folks at Forest City Community Church in Dresden graciously opened their doors to us and gave us a place to work on a moment's notice. Later in the year, St. Cuthbert's Presbyterian Church in Hamilton made space available to the editing team. It was conveniently located near the highway and the train station. The use of both of these facilities was greatly appreciated.

Editing Team

Judee Archer Green, Convener of the Week of Prayer for Christian Unity Writing Team, Presbyterian Church in Canada.

Mary Marrocco, Associate Secretary of Faith and Witness Commission, Canadian Council of Churches, Roman Catholic.

Richard T. Vander Vaart, Member of the Week of Prayer for Christian Unity Writing Team, Christian Reformed Church in North America—Canada.

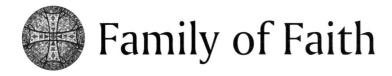
Family of Faith

Steven Ottományi, 2007
reprinted with permission of the Friars of the Atonement

Lord Jesus Christ, who rose from death,
Our spirit's life, our spirit's breath:
You show the way that leads to peace,
Where anger sleeps, where hatreds cease.

O Key of David, open wide
The doors now blocked by human pride.
Come, change our hearts, make clear our need
To follow where your will shall lead.

And still, O Lord, you walk our way;
You walk with us both night and day.
You call us, Lord, in love to be
A sign of hope, of unity.

So lead us, Lord, to live and claim
All that it means to bear your name.
Now make of us one family
Of faith, of hope, of charity.

Copyright © 2007, National Association of Pastoral Musicians and Friars of the Atonement.

All rights reserved.

Family of Faith

1. Lord Jesus Christ, who rose from death, Our spirit's life, our spirit's breath: You show the way that leads to peace, Where anger sleeps, where hatreds cease.
2. O Key of David, open wide The doors now blocked by human pride. Come, change our hearts, make clear our need To follow where your will shall lead.
3. And still, O Lord, you walk our way; You walk with us both night and day. You call us, Lord, in love to be A sign of hope, of unity.
4. So lead us, Lord, to live and claim All that it means to bear your name. Now make of us one family Of faith, of hope, of charity.

Text: Steven Ottományi, b. 1973. © National Association of Pastoral Musicians and Friars of the Atonement. All rights reserved.
Tune: PROSPECT, LM, W. Walter, *Southern Harmony*, 1835; harm. S. Ottományi, 2007

That All May Be One in Christ

Ricky Manalo, CSP
reprinted with permission of the Friars of the Atonement

Refrain

O God, make us one as we come to the table,
One in Spirit and in truth.
Now you have given us bread for the world,
That all may be one in Christ
and all may be one in You.

Verse One

In the vision we behold
You have called us into Your home.
Many stories, ancient and new,
make us one in You.

Verse Two

Through the rising of Your Son,
You have conquered sin and death.
Feed us with the Bread of Life;
Make us one in Christ.

Verse Three

As You breathe upon the earth,
Send Your Spirit into our hearts.
Heal divisions, fashion anew
the hope we find in You.

That All May Be One In Christ

In celebration of the Centenary of the Week of Prayer for Christian Unity

Spanish verses by Rodolfo López
Vietnamese verses by Nguyen Dinh Dien

Ricky Manalo, CSP
Arranged by Gerard Chiusano

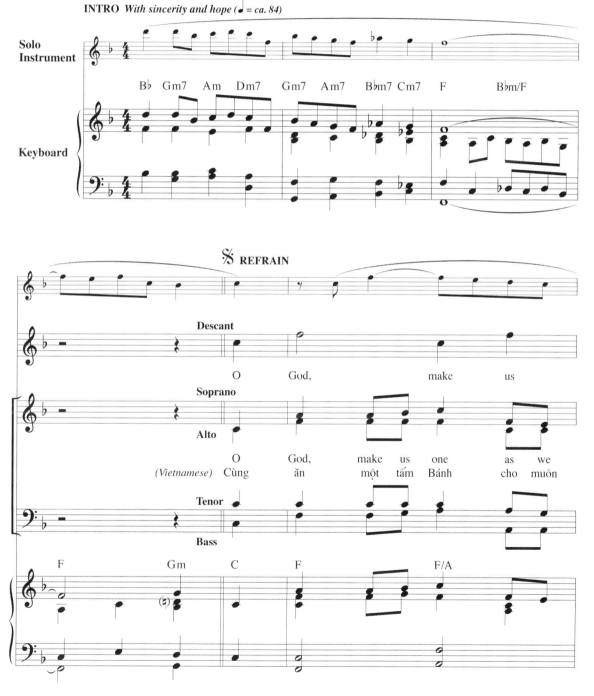

© 2007, National Association of Pastoral Musicians and Friars of the Atonement. All rights reserved.

Subject Index

Afghanistan 8, 151
AIDS 165–166
Angell, Charles 26
Anglican orders, nullity of 21
Apostle of Christian Unity (*see* Couturier, Abbé Paul)
Apostles' Creed 84
Archbishop of Canterbury 9, 15, 20
Association for the Promotion of the Unity of Christendom 14
Athenagoras, Orthodox patriarch 109

Baptismal life 102, 148
Baptismal promises, renewal of 101
Beaudoin, Dom Lambert 20
Benedict XV, Pope 18
Benedictine Monks of Unity 27
Berdyaev, Nicholas 19, 21–22
Berlin Wall, collapse of 132
Blessing
    after a meal 141–142
    of bread 133–134, 135
    of salt 135
Body of Christ 8, 13, 17, 108, 120, 145
Bread of Life 64

Canadian Catholic Conference (*see* Canadian Conference of Catholic Bishops)
Canadian Conference of Catholic Bishops 93, 130
Canadian Council of Churches 7, 8, 12, 53, 54, 73, 130
    as originator of prayer 101, 109, 110, 114, 115, 116, 117, 118, 120, 124, 125, 131, 132, 136, 141, 145, 146, 153, 155, 157, 158, 161, 164, 165, 168, 169
    Commission on Faith and Witness 11
    Faith and Order Commission 54
Centre for Ecumenism, Montreal 54, 73
Centre Unité Chrétienne (Lyon) 33, 53–54
    as originator of prayer 62, 63, 65, 67, 68, 69, 96
Chair of Peter 53
Challenges of celebrating in wartime 43, 45, 47
Change of heart 66, 69–70
Charity 59, 68
Church, nature of the 56, 62, 67, 85
Churches
    Anglican 8, 9, 13, 14, 15, 16, 17, 18, 20, 25, 29, 43, 50, 53, 84, 93, 109, 142
    Baptist 14, 25, 77, 142
    called to repentance 39, 40
    Christian Reformed 130
    Congregationalist 14, 31, 46, 77
    Evangelical Lutheran (*see* Lutheran)
    gifts of the 41, 42
    importance of visible unity of 23–25
    in communist countries 59
    Lutheran 9, 10, 18, 25, 77, 93, 96
    Methodist 14, 25, 31, 46, 61, 77
    Old Catholic 25, 77
    Orthodox 8, 9, 14, 22, 25, 27, 28, 44, 50, 53, 55, 76, 109, 133, 142
    Presbyterian 14, 25, 31, 46, 77, 93, 142, 165
    Reformed 25, 29, 77, 140, 142
    Roman Catholic 8, 9, 14, 15, 16, 18, 20, 27, 30, 33, 43, 50, 53, 59, 69, 73, 78, 84, 93, 97, 109, 123, 142
    United 9, 25, 93, 142
Coalitions 9
Common date, week of Prayer 42–43, 44

Common loyalty to Christ 45

Common worship 60, 62

Complacency, sin of 26

Conversion 20, 30, 53, 151, 155–156

Cooperation 98

Council of Trent 62

Couturier, Abbé Paul 7, 26–31, 33, 53, 57, 69, 168

Cranny, Titus 16

Creed 74, 84, 102, 124

Cross 38–39, 54, 76, 100, 116, 151–152, 155, 163, 167

Cultural issues 53, 73, 93–94, 102–103, 107–108, 129, 151

Curtis, Geoffrey 20

Davidson, Randall (Dr) 20

De Lisle, Ambrose Phillips 14

Deliverance from human motivations that limit 59, 66

DeLubac, Henri 28

Didache 67, 77

Dignity of the person 95, 121

Dionysius, St. 65

Disunity, suffering caused by 17, 21, 66, 68, 74, 147

Divisions
> as hindrance to work of God 38, 59
> personal responsibility for 38, 68, 80
> scandal of 7, 24, 38
> theological 46, 55, 56, 57

Dix, Dom Gregory 29

Doxology 153

Ecumenical commitment, renewal of 145, 148

Ecumenical movement 12, 13, 19, 61, 73–74, 76, 79, 93, 107, 109, 129

Ecumenism
> as Christ's own mandate 28
> as essential to Gospel 107

> as mutual understanding and acceptance 130
> as unity in the body of Christ 129
> spiritual 22, 27, 29, 30
> spirituality of 28, 29

Education (as part of ecumenical work) 75, 95, 99, 108, 110, 129

Edwards, Jonathan 14

Eucharist 9, 10, 133, 145

Evangelical Alliance 14

Evangelical Youth, Germany 86

Expo '67 73, 87–89, 97

Faith and Order 19, 45, 47, 48, 53–54, 55, 56, 59, 60, 68

Faithful witnesses 56

Family of God 81

Fellowship of St. Alban and St. Sergius 9

Fourth World Conference on Faith and Order 73

Freedom 90–91

Friars of the Atonement (*see also* Graymoor) 7, 11, 17, 26

Friendship, personal (as ecumenical sphere) 10, 19, 20, 21, 65, 93, 136

Fundamentals, The 15

Gardiner, Robert H. 23–26

Gathering the scattered 67, 77, 80, 164

Gratitude 82

Graymoor 7, 11, 16–17, 53, 86
> (as originator of prayer) 95, 99, 101, 104, 100, 110, 111, 117, 119, 121, 122, 123, 125, 131, 137, 138, 140, 143, 148, 155, 156, 163, 164, 167

Halifax, Viscount 21

Healing
> of divisions 45, 55, 64, 66, 88, 151
> of sickness 165–166

Heller, Dagmar 15

Henry VIII, King 17

HIV (*see* AIDS)

Hodgson, Leonard 31, 42, 44, 45, 46, 47, 48, 49

Holy Ghost (*see* Holy Spirit)

Holy Spirit 12, 13, 41, 45, 48, 64, 66, 86, 95, 96, 97, 99, 137, 138–139, 141, 157
    unifying power of 14, 94, 123

Hooft, Willem Adolph Visser 't 33

Hope 7, 87, 88, 103, 107

Hospitality as ministry of unity 24, 76, 136, 139–140

Image of God 70, 75, 158, 165–166

Incarnation 151, 161–162, 168

Inculturation 129

Indifference 65

Inner life 63

Intercommunion 63

International Missionary Council 19

Intransigence, dangers of 42

Iona Community 86

Iraq 8, 151

Jesson, Nicholas 15, 20

Jews 18

John Paul II, Pope 151

John XXIII, Pope 53

Joint Committee of the World Council of Churches and the Pontifical Commission for the Promotion of Christian Unity 11

Jones, Rev. Spencer 17, 18, 19

Judaism 29

Justice
    as basis for society 103, 109
    of God 78, 91

Kierkegaard, Soren 29–30

Kingdom (of God) 110

Knowledge in the service of unity 60, 62

Kooiman, Peter 48

Lambeth Conference of Anglican Bishops 15

Lamp, The 17

Laypeople 10

Lee, Frederick George 14

Leo XIII, Pope 15

Lewis, Stephen 165–166

Liberalism 15

Life and Work movement 19

Light 86, 119, 154, 155, 159

Litanies 64, 66
    for reconciliation and unity 99, 111, 114, 118, 155
    of petition 80, 98, 137
    of repentance 79, 104, 132–133, 144, 163
    of thanksgiving 66, 79, 131, 142

Liturgy of St. James 86

Liturgy of St. John Chrysostom 68

Lord's Prayer, as prototype of Christian prayer 28

Love
    as path to unity 24, 91, 98, 136, 159
    role of 42, 54, 68, 69

Lund 55, 56, 59, 61, 109

Lyon 27–29, 53

Malines conversations 20

Maruthas of Tancrit, Liturgy 86

Meditations 70, 78, 83

Mercer, Robert 26

Mercier, Cardinal 20–21, 27

Milestones in ecumenical work 109

Mission, as impetus for unity 17, 19, 23, 69, 73, 90

Modernist Controversy 15

Monastery, invisible 29

Moon, walk (1969) 93

Mother Teresa's Daily Prayer 117

Mystery of Christ 58

Name, new 82

National Council of Churches 7

Nedtotchine, Father 28

Neighbour, presence of God in 95, 117, 167

Nelson. J. Robert 61

New Delhi Assembly 73

Newman, John Henry 14, 16

Newness 82, 83

Non-Christians 140–141

Novalis, collaboration with 74, 108

Octave of Christian Unity 11
    changing understanding of 11

Octave of Prayer for the Unity of the Church
    18

Octave of Prayer for Unity of Christians 23

Olympics 102–103

Opening and receptive listening 59, 95

Orthodoxy 21–22, 25, 27, 28

Papacy, primacy of 17

Patience 56

Peace 70, 78, 81, 84, 85, 86, 103, 110, 121,
158–161
    and justice 19, 158–159
    and unity of the church 37, 39, 65, 70,
    76

Peers, Michael G. 10

Pentecost 11

Perfume, liturgical use of 168

Perroy, Father 28

Persecution 55, 148

Pius IX, Pope 15

Pius X, Pope 18

Plan of Union 9

Pluralism 98

Portal, Fernand 21

Prairie Centre for Ecumenism 15

Praise 82

Prayer
    after war 49
    and community 8
    body of Christ 8
    as central to work of ecumenism 39, 129
    as Christ's prayer 82
    centrality of, for unity 7, 24, 27, 33–34,
    58, 73, 169
    intercessory, importance of 58

Prayers 40, 60, 65, 67–68, 69, 70–71, 78, 81,
82, 86, 88, 96, 100, 101, 103, 110, 113,
115, 116, 117, 120, 125, 132, 135, 138,
141, 158, 159, 168
    call to worship 111, 143, 167
    confession 79, 99, 101, 113, 131, 132,
    144, 156, 162
    dismissal 113, 164
    for individual churches: Anglicans and
    Old Catholics 77; Baptists, Congrega-
    tionalists and Methodists 77, 142; Free
    Churches 142; Lutherans, Presbyterians
    and Reformed 77, 142; Orthodox and
    Eastern Churches 76, 142; Other Chris-
    tians 77; Pentecostal movements 142;
    Protestant and Evangelical 142; Reli-
    gious Societies of Friends 142; Roman
    Catholic 76, 78, 142; United Church of
    Canada 142
    intercessory 38, 42, 45, 50–51, 54–55,
    59–60, 62–63, 64, 80, 84, 89, 95, 98–99,
    123, 134, 137, 140, 142, 168
    missioning 100, 125, 146, 154,
    thanksgiving 41, 45, 66

Proclamation of faith 146

Profession of faith (*see* Apostles' Creed)

Psychology of Christian unity 27, 30

Pugin, A.W. 14

Pulpit of the Cross, The 16

Purification 66

Ramsey, Dr. Michael 109

Reconciled to God 78, 130, 155, 158–161

Reconciliation of differences 56, 57, 70–71, 77, 86, 90

Reformation 65

Relevance 93

Religious Societies of Friends 25, 143

Reparation 63

Repentance 38, 54, 79, 121–122, 131, 156, 163

Revelation, Book of 147

Revivalist movement 14

Romanticism 15

Rome, reunion with 17

Rouse, Ruth 14–15

Runcie, Robert 9, 10

Ryan, Thomas CSP 9

Saints Peter and Paul, feast of 11

Salt 135

Sayers, Dorothy 84

Schultz, Roger 29

Scotland 14

Scripture
- and the mystery of Christ 57
- as common foundation 57

Scriptures
- love for 58
- return to the 57

Second Vatican Council 7, 33, 73, 78, 89

Separation, Christian East and West 65

September 11, 2001 151

Sins, acknowledging our 62, 63, 68

Sisters of the Reformed Community 29

Social action/justice 9, 10, 93, 95, 97

Social change, church's response to 15

Social gospel movement 15

Social issues 115, 116, 123, 129, 165–166

Society of the Atonement, origins of 16–17

Solidarity 96, 108, 120, 123

Special Commission on the Place of the Orthodox churches in the World Council of Churches 9

Spencer, Ignatius 14

Stewart, James Haldae (Rev) 14

Suffering, human 24, 32, 87, 107, 137, 156, 157, 165, 167

Syriac liturgy 159–161

Taizé 29, 107

Teaching 75

Technological change 15

Thanksgiving 86, 141
- after meal (*see* Blessing after meal)
- for ecumenical progress 46, 49

Thurian, Max 29

Tomkins, Oliver S. 48, 50, 55, 56, 60, 68

Transformation of the world 94, 103, 122, 139

Trinity 68, 81, 116, 129–130, 144, 153

Understanding between East and West 50

Unity 67, 75, 77, 95, 96, 103, 123, 132
- as reconciliation to the Catholic Church 69
- diversity in 8, 93, 125, 129
- in diversity 40, 41, 108, 121
- of all people 78, 81, 82
- of Christ and the church 58, 73, 168

Universality of Christ 67, 95

Van der Leeuw, Professor 48

Vision 147

Visualization 70

Water 151, 155

Waterloo Declaration 9

Wattson, Joseph 16

Wattson, Lewis Thomas 16

Wattson, Paul (Rev) 7, 15, 16–18

Week of Prayer for Christian Unity 8, 11, 13, 17, 18
- and Judaism 29
- growth of 28–29, 31, 33, 44, 56
- 100th anniversary of 8

White, Mother Lurana 16, 17

Witness 122, 123

Word of God 143–144

World Council of Churches 7, 11, 19, 48, 50,
        53, 54
        as originator of prayer 50, 55, 56, 59, 60,
        62, 64, 65, 66, 67, 68, 70, 75, 76, 78, 82,
        89, 90

World Missionary Conference 1910 19

World War I 24

World War II 31–33, 48

Worship
        importance of 63
        Protestant 9

Youth ministry 139–140

Scripture Index

Genesis 22.1-18	91	John 1.1	143
Genesis 4.9	95	John 6. 56	38
Exodus 2.23-3.12	90	John 8. 32	90
Deuteronomy 6.6-9	75	John 8.31-36	90
		John 10.10	110
Psalm 19.7-14	136	John 14.27	15, 40
Psalm 34		John 15.8-17	136
Psalm 34.1-10	116	John 16. 12-15	111
Psalm 57	101	John 16.8	62
Psalm 95	110	John 17.21	7, 10, 27, 28, 29, 169
Psalm 96	83	John 19.30	97
Psalm 96.1	83	John 19.34	151
Psalm 98	136	John 20. 19-23	78
Psalm 99	110	Acts 1.18	132
Psalm 97	110	Acts 2.33	97
Isaiah 12	82	Romans 8. 14-25	91
Isaiah 40.1-11	91	Romans 8.19	110
Isaiah 55.6	169	1 Corinthians 10.23-33	91
Isaiah 61.1-4	116	1 Corinthians 12.3b-13	111
Isaiah 61.1-4, 11	90	1 Corinthians 12.12	8
Isaiah 61.8-11	136	1 Corinthians 12.26	167
Jeremiah 34.8-17	91	1 Corinthians 9. 24-25	102
Ezekiel 36.24-28	90	2 Corinthians 1.3-7	87
Ezekiel 37.27	85	2 Corinthians 3.1-6	90
Hosea 2.16-23	85	2 Corinthians 3.17	90
		2 Corinthians 4.7-15	116
Micah 6.6-8	136	2 Corinthians 5.19	90
Matthew 28.16-20	116	2 Corinthians 5.20	78
Mark 7.31-37	165	Galatians 4.1-7, 5.1	90
Mark 8.31-35	91	Galatians 5.1	90
Luke 1.46-55	132	Galatians 5.13-26	91
Luke 1.67-79	132	Galatians 5.22-6.2	136
Luke 15. 1-10	136	Ephesians 1.2	111
Luke 15.11-32	165	Ephesians 1.3	111
Luke 24.13-35	165		

1 Timothy 1.15	133
1 Timothy 2.5-6	133
1 Timothy 3.16	133
2 Timothy 3.14-17	75
Hebrews 13.2	76
1 Peter 1.3-9	87
1 Peter 4.7-11	94
Revelation 19.4-9	136
Revelation 21	146
Revelation 21.1-7	85
Revelation 21.3	85
Revelation 21.5	146
Revelation 21.5	82
Revelation 3.12	82
Revelation 3.7-13	82
Revelation 5. 6-14	83
Revelations 21.3	110